MORMON
AND *Single*
...again

By David F. Clark, M.A.

Publishing

ISBN   0-9771108-0-X

First Printing, 2005

Printed in the United States of America

MORMON
AND *Single*
...again

Dedication

This book is dedicated to my daughters. I am overwhelmingly grateful for them. Their love lifts and inspires me every day.

Acknowledgements

So many people contributed to this book (many without their knowledge or consent) that I cannot possibly name them all. In reverse alphabetical order, however, Sue, Roberta, Rick, Pat, Missy, Mike, Melissa, Holly, Helena, Gary, Chris, Cherrie, Bob, Barbara, Anne, Andy, and Andrea all selflessly donated their editorial efforts. I thank them. Any grammatical errors are solely their responsibility.

Special thanks go to PJ Cervantes, for his twisted mind is responsible for the cover design. I would also like to thank everyone who took the time to share the tales of their dating adventures with me (especially Alison - wow). You saved me the trouble of having to live it all myself.

Finally, thank you to everyone I've ever dated. Whether our time together was wonderful or disastrous, I learned something about myself and gained a desire to write it all down.

Table of Contents

Introduction

When I was sealed to my beautiful, young bride in the Las Vegas Temple, I never expected to be dating again. This was because we planned to be together for eternity. Well, eternity turned out to be 9 years, 11 months, and 14 days.

To say I was surprised is an understatement. I couldn't have been more shocked if I'd gone to a ward party that started on time and did not feature a single Jell-O product. They say that when tragedy strikes, you can either laugh or you can cry. Well, I did plenty of both, but I thought I would just share the laughter. After six years, I've realized that my sense of humor has helped me survive and adapt to the strange, new world of SAMs (Single Again Mormons, not Surface to Air Missiles).

Being divorced and LDS is somewhat like being a jockey who suddenly gains 300 pounds. You just don't feel like you fit in anymore. As you read this, I hope you will realize that you're not alone as a divorced Mormon. Unfortunately, there are now plenty of us, and we're all alone together. Better yet, we're simply all together. Like the pioneers who crossed the plains through weather, sickness, and pain, you can take comfort in the fact that you're not the only one losing toes to frostbite. Or something like that.

I hope you enjoy this lighthearted look at the heart-wrenching trials in your life. Keep in mind as you read that many of the stories and examples will apply to both genders. I leave it up to you to apply them accordingly (liken all non-scripture unto you). You may even find plural pronouns that refer to singular male or female nouns. It's not that I'm unaware of the litany of grammatical rules governing gender, voice, and consistency, it's just that I don't care.

So You're Single Again...
Now What?

Daily Life

Whatever the reason for your divorce, you are now single. You may feel relief, anguish, joy, anger, and a million other emotions, perhaps simultaneously. When you get right down to it though, your daily life is different than it was before. There are advantages and disadvantages to being single. On the plus side, you don't have to share dessert with anyone ("I'll just have a bite of yours"); on the down side, if you don't take out the trash or empty the lint trap, it simply doesn't get done.

> *Editor's Note:* It turns out that there's this screen in clothes dryers that sucks lint and single socks out of the tumbler. Apparently, if you don't clean it out regularly, the dryer will stop working. The lint in the trap may even catch fire. I don't want to say how I know this, but I would like to make it clear that lint is highly flammable, so if this wasn't your chore before, make sure it is now.

Taking stock of the reality of your situation is an important first step towards the rest of your miserable, lonely life, branded as an outcast of normal LDS society. Just kidding. Remember that when life closes a door, it often opens a window to dump lemons on you, so you can make lemonade and fill a glass half full while looking for a silver lining on the gathering clouds. I recommend that you begin by making a list of all the pros and cons regarding your breakup. If you were abandoned, you probably have a head full of cons. If you did the leaving, you're probably skewed toward the pros. I've included a list of popular items below to help get you started on your own list.

Pros	Cons
You can listen to whatever music you like at whatever volume you choose.	She took all the CDs with her.
You get to pick the TV program, and you can watch it while you eat on the couch.	You have no TV, couch, or food.
You don't have to clean up after anyone else.	You have to kill all your own spiders and open all your own jars.
You can eat ice cream right out of the carton.	You pretend to like salad on dinner dates.
Hygiene (including shaving) is optional.	Smelling like a yak won't make a good first impression.

Pros	Cons
Anyone you meet could turn out to be that "special someone."	You have to look nice when the plumber arrives because he might be single and cute.
You can buy the dog you've always wanted.	Dogs don't cook.
The toilet seat stays down.	You have to plunge it yourself.
You win every argument.	You find yourself arguing with your cat.
You can eat cookies in bed because there's no one in bed with you to complain.	There's no one in bed with you to complain.
You can squeeze the toothpaste tube in the middle.	It doesn't really matter if you have fresh, minty breath.
You're free to date now.	You're free to date now.

Church

    The first few times you go to church during and after your divorce, you may feel a little awkward. And by a little awkward, I mean you will feel as though you are walking around naked with a rabid wolverine on your head, pretending that nothing is wrong. Don't worry about it. The feeling passes in a few short years, and eventually you will feel as though the imaginary wolverine on your head is rather docile and friendly.

Contributing to your feelings of comfort and belonging are the lessons you will enjoy each week in Priesthood and Relief Society. They will remind you that you're right on track with your eternal goals and strengthen you to face another week of your new reality. The lesson plans for a typical month are:

1st Sunday - *No Success Can Compensate for Failure in the Home;*
2nd Sunday - *Being a Worthy Husband and Father*
           (or Wife and Mother);
3rd Sunday - *Families Can be Together Forever;*
4th Sunday - *No Success Can Compensate for Failure in the Home.*

These four lessons will be repeated each month. I recommend sitting in the back row where no one will notice your quiet sobs. Whatever you do, don't contribute to the lesson. You may be well-intentioned, but your comment or question will always result in an awkward silence and draw attention to your tear-stained face. Here's a simple test. If "So what happens if your husband cheats on you and leaves you for his twenty-year-old secretary?" seems like a reasonable question to put before the class then you're probably not ready to participate in the lesson – especially if the lesson is on tithing.

If you are attending a family ward, you will find that you are the only single person in your ward. Each family ward is allowed one single person and you are it. This means that you will be called to be the single adult representative in your ward, which is roughly the equivalent of being called as the weekly root canal patient.

You were called to this position so you would feel obligated to attend the stake activities where you will have the opportunity to interact with others in your same situation, your peers. The first few times you do this, you will think to yourself, "These are my peers?" as you run screaming from the room. This is a natural reaction. No one wants to belong to this group at first, but your will to maintain your self-respect will be gradually worn away until you accept your fate.

If you're over thirty and thinking of attending a "mature" singles ward, don't bother. I don't think they really exist. And like UFO's, the Loch Ness Monster, Elvis, and fat-free ice cream, some mysteries are simply best left unexplored.

If you are under 31 and decide to attend a young singles ward, you will be thrown into a maelstrom of dances, activities, meetings, and other social interactions with a wide variety of individuals with whom you have nothing in common because you are divorced. Actually, it only feels that way. You will soon realize that the problem is not your divorced status, it's the fact that everyone else is shallow, self-absorbed, and judgmental. What you won't realize is that it only seems that way because you're still bitter from your failed marriage. The problem is, in fact, you and your attitude.

So how do you deal with this problem (your

attitude or everyone else's shortcomings– depending upon your perspective)? It involves putting aside your discomfort and engaging others in positive social interactions until you're able to overcome your bitterness and allow meaningful relationships into your life again. This is known more commonly as "going through the motions."

As you go through the motions, you will notice others doing the same. Introduce yourself and focus your interactions on them because there is little risk of a confrontation (or even a DTR – covered in later chapters) if you're both just going through the motions. Eventually, you will outgrow this strategy (or simply turn 31 and get kicked out of the ward), but for now it will protect your fragile emotions from people who live in the real world.

When you start to lose that sense of self-consciousness and begin to feel like you might actually fit in somewhere, it's time to start bringing your children to the singles ward with you. Now don't go blaming other ward members for their reactions to your children. They're young, childless, and often don't know how to respond to these short humans. Comments will range from, "I didn't know you had kids," (in the same consoling tone your parents used when they told you your dog died) to, "How did that happen?" or "So what do you do with them?" I recommend that you have some canned, zippy responses ready for those bold enough to set themselves up in such an awkward manner. If you're a woman, your best response is, "Oh, I'm not positive that they're even mine."

Try this fun social psychology experiment. Show up to Sacrament Meeting fifteen minutes early. You will, of course, be the only one besides the bishop in the building this early. Take a seat with your children in the middle of the center pew. Fourteen minutes later, as the room begins to fill with the early birds, watch how the rows furthest from you fill first. Later arrivals are forced to sit closer and closer to you until, just as the ten foot barrier is about to be broken, someone opens the screen to the overflow seating in the gym.

You are now sitting in the center of the child zone, a perfectly formed circle which is empty of all life except you and your children (of course, others with children may occupy this zone without fear). It is as though you have been so busy mowing lawns in the hot sun that you haven't had time to shower for the past month. I often wonder if young singles are under the impression that children are contagious and that you can get pregnant by sitting too close to one. I would like to state emphatically and for the record that this is not the case (unless you touch a crayon, coloring book, or soggy Cheerio).

Of course, I am exaggerating the way that nemamomos (never married Mormons) will react to the knowledge that you have children. Many of the people in your singles ward have siblings that are the same age as your children, and feel very comfortable around them. These people are often called to the Primary, and they will feel like an island sanctuary in a sea of nemamomos.

Do not judge nemamomos too harshly. They

simply have a different set of life experiences than you do and need time to adjust their paradigm to see the world from another's point of view (as do you). Following is an actual message left on my voicemail by a nemamomo whom I dated for 30 days (no more, no less – that was her policy). She was pretty uncomfortable with the fact that I had two daughters. This call came approximately one year after we stopped dating.

"Hey, Dave. Well, good news. The Bishop of my new ward called me to the Primary a few months ago, and I've been able to overcome my fear of children. In fact, I actually like them now. Also, I still haven't found anybody better than you. So I have a proposal to make, literally. Give me a call if you're sick of dating and want to get married."

I know. It's so romantic, it makes you want to cry. Of course she was being facetious (I think). While she had indeed given up hope of finding anything better (there's a dark day), I sensed that she had not yet completed her contributions to this book. So we decided not to enter into a loveless marriage. This bold decision has allowed her to continue her hobby of dating social misfits of epic proportions (present company excluded, I'm assured), thus generating some of the most entertaining stories within these pages.

The point, however, is that whether you go to a family ward or a singles ward, you may feel as though you are surrounded by people with whom you have nothing in common. But in reality you're surrounded by brothers and sisters with whom you have everything in common except for a few life experiences, so if you focus on the similarities instead of the differences, you'll soon feel right at home as you realize that… blah, blah, blah. Sorry. I almost forgot that this book isn't like that.

Family Gatherings

Is it Christmas already? My, how time flies. Planning to spend time with your family because your kids are with the ex? Here's my recommendation. Don't. Just don't. Whether your family yells and screams, or hugs and sings during the holidays, it's going to drive you insane for the first couple of years.

You'll see your siblings with their loving spouses and happy kids basking in their love for one another, and the happiness and joy of these loved ones who mean so much to you will make you want to vomit. Specifically, you will want to vomit on them to try to suck some of the joy out of their holiday. Then you will want to key their cars as you leave.

I have a couple of recommendations on this topic. First, consider getting some anger management counseling because you're out of control with the vomiting and keying. Second, treat yourself to a few days on the beach or in the mountains instead of sentencing yourself to family time during the holidays. If you're going to be alone on Christmas, you might as well enjoy it. When you go to the family party, you're still alone, you're just alone around a bunch of people whose lives are reminding you of everything that you've recently lost. When you go to the beach, you're alone with the wonders of nature, which promote introspection, healing, and attractive people in swimsuits. Stop feeling sorry for yourself and have an adventure.

You can interact with your family members individually in order to maintain and strengthen those important relationships. You're not ready to deal with seeing them in all their familial glory though. You need to be a little removed in time from the unexpected transition that took your Cinderella fairy tale and dropped in Jason or Justin (whichever one wears the hockey mask, not the one in the boy band – he gives me the creeps).

If this means that you can't attend Family Home Evenings with your family of origin, that's okay. The church offers special Family Home Evenings each week (I think they're on Mondays) for members who are single, and remember, you're now single. We'll get to that later. For now, let's take your temperature and see if you're ready to meet new people, or if you need to keep hiding inside your house.

Are You Ready to Date Again?

A few weeks after my divorce, I flew to California to spend a couple of days on the beach and try to get my bearings. I ran into an old friend with whom I had worked years earlier. We spent an afternoon together, and I asked if she wanted to have dinner that evening.

"I can't," she said. "I would really love to, but I just can't. You're not ready, and I would just be taking advantage of you if I started dating you now."

Not ready? I couldn't imagine what she meant by that, so I posed the question to her.

"David," she continued. "I've always thought you were a keeper, but right now you're an emotional wreck. You shouldn't be dating, and I'm not going to be the one to hurt you first."

"I'm not an emotional wreck," I protested, fighting back the tears. "I just... excuse me, I have to use the restroom." After composing myself, I returned and resumed my argument. "I'm not an emotional wreck. I just (excuse me), I am just (excuse me), I'm just adjusting to a different lifestyle after being deserted by the woman that I've loved for fifteen years, so I think it's okay if I'm a little upset, and I might need a moment here or there to compose myself as I

reflect on the pain of the knife sticking out of my back, but it certainly doesn't mean that I'm an emotional wreck."

There was a long pause as we just looked at each other.

"Okay," I conceded. "But just because I'm an emotional wreck, doesn't mean we can't date."

There was another long pause.

"Thank you for your honesty."

She smiled. "There's no hurry, David. Deal with your divorce before you try to find a new relationship."

One of the first things you need to assess when you become single, is your relative level of emotional and mental health. You don't want to make any major decisions in your life, and you probably don't even want to start dating until you've dealt with a lot of the emotions that are left over from your divorce.

Fortunately, I've developed an assessment tool that will measure whether you're ready to rejoin society. I refer to this tool as the Bitterness Scale, or BS. Answer the questions honestly, so you can get an accurate measurement of your BS score.

1. When you meet an attractive member of the opposite sex, do you think:
   a) Wow! What an attractive person. I'd sure like to get to know her better.
   b) That person must be very happy and popular and would never want to have anything to do with me.
   c) Just look at you, standing there, thinking you're so hot. You can't fool me. I know that you're really a raving psychotic lunatic trying to suck someone into your emotional games. You're nothing more than a Venus flytrap waiting to crush my heart like a dried up, old leaf for your personal pleasure.
   d) I hate you. I hate everyone. Leave me alone.

2. When you go with friends to see a pleasant, little romantic comedy, do you think:
   a) What a pleasant, little romantic comedy.
   b) How depressing. This is just like my life, only without the happy ending.
   c) What a stupid idea for a movie. No need to come up with an original idea. The guy and girl fall in love and get together at the end after a hilarious series of misunderstandings. Surprise! Ten bucks for a ticket and eight bucks for enough popcorn to feed a small country. What a waste. I'm going home.
   d) I hate this movie. I hate everyone. Leave me alone.

3. When a love song comes on the radio, do you:
    a) Sing along with a smile on your face and love in your heart.
    b) Roll your eyes, shake your head, and change the station.
    c) Calmly pull over to the side of the road, engage your hazard lights, curl into the fetal position on the front seat, and sob quietly until the feeling passes.
    d) Hate the song. Hate the artist. Hate the DJ. Start screaming like a lunatic at the radio, ranting a query to the universe about why every song is a stupid love song and why you're the only one who's not allowed to be happy.

4. On your birthday, do you:
    a) Wake up smiling and have a great day, knowing that you've earned another year's worth of experience on this great journey that is life.
    b) Mope to yourself about how your life is nothing like you expected and that you're going to have to make some changes.
    c) Snap at everyone you meet during the day and give an extra glare to anyone who appears to be more than ten years younger than you.
    d) Stay in bed all day, hating everyone. Give yourself a bonus point if you leave bed only to burn little effigies of that person who ruined your life and made it the living hell that it is today.

5. When you pray, is it for:
   a) God's will, whatever that may be, to be played out in your life and the strength to endure whatever trials he has in mind for you to facilitate your growth as an individual. This prayer includes many thanks.
   b) Guidance and strength to navigate troubled waters until the peace and joy that must surely be just around the corner finally comes to save you.
   c) Someone or something to remove everything bad from your life, replacing it with all your dreams come true, including, of course, your knight in shining armor or beautiful princess.
   d) God to smite your enemies and put you in a position to mock and deride them as they suffer through a satisfying example of poetic justice worthy of Dante.

6. On Sundays, you attend church meetings:
   a) until the meeting block ends and you've helped put away the chairs.
   b) until someone starts giving a lesson or talk on families (every week) and how no success can compensate for failure in the home.
   c) Unless there's a game on that you want to see. When you do attend, you sit in the back, don't socialize, and don't make eye contact with anyone in the bishopric. If they "drop by" to visit, you'll talk to them on the porch, but won't invite them in (even if they have treats).
   d) Attend? You drive past a church on your way home from work. You do remember that you don't like your bishop and life isn't fair, so you're not going.

7. When you run into your ex-spouse at the mall with her new boyfriend, do you:
   a) Greet them, chat pleasantly for a few minutes, and then continue with your shopping.
   b) Duck into the nearest store, hope they don't see you, and try not to look awkward when they happen to wander in and see you pretending to shop (especially if you were trying to hide in a lingerie store).
   c) Tell the security guard that they look a lot like the "mall cop killers" you saw on America's Most Wanted last night. Better call for backup.
   d) Scream, bang your head against a wall, and confront them, informing the new companion of the betrayal tendencies of your ex-spouse. After the fight is broken up, sob quietly and think hateful thoughts as you're being taken to jail (or the hospital).

8. When you start dating someone new, do you:
   a) Slowly build a relationship of mutual trust and affection.
   b) Consciously hope against hope that you've finally found the one member of the opposite sex who isn't a malicious, psychotic freak that's going to make it their mission in life to bring you emotional pain.
   c) Assume that they are eventually going to break up with you, and break up with them first.
   d) Hate them before they can hate you. Start arguing with them twenty minutes into the first date, blaming them for something that your ex-spouse did to you, call them by your ex's name, and fumble through your purse or pockets for your medication or pepper spray.

9. You watch the evening news because:
    a) You like to be aware of current events and try to find the silver lining in every seemingly negative story.
    b) It's a necessary part of being a contributing member of society, and you find that you learn something new about yourself and the world around you each night if you have the proper attitude.
    c) It's a distraction that will suck thirty minutes of your life away during which you won't have to think about how horrible your life is or about the people who ruined it.
    d) Seeing other people suffer makes you feel a little bit better about the tortured, embittered existence that is your life.

10. On Friday nights:
    a) You typically spend time with friends or go out on dates, but you're content to spend the evening alone if plans don't materialize during the week. You may also enjoy spending the time with your children. If you're using the children as an excuse to avoid dating, however, score this question as a 2.5.
    b) You try to find a date and feel a little insecure if you spend the evening alone. You may spend extra time at work to avoid facing this feeling.
    c) Your mother calls because she knows you'll be home.
    d) You sit at home writing hate mail to talk show therapists, eating ice cream right out of the carton, watching the same episode of SportsCenter three times in a row, and mentally reliving every relationship you've ever had (both real and imaginary).

Each answer has a value between one and four: count every "a" as one point, "b" as two points, "c" as three points, and "d" as four points. If you were too upset by the content of the question to be able to answer, count that as ten points. Go ahead and add up your scores from the ten questions above and check them against the scale below.

1-9: So math isn't your strong suit. That's okay. I'm sure you have a number of other qualities that more than make up for your inability to add a series of single-digit numbers together.

10: A very good score. Unfortunately, you're either a pathological liar or simply so deep in denial that you're watching seven fat cows and seven skinny cows swimming past you towards the pyramids. Denial is not a bad thing; it protects us from reality. Reality's not going away though (sorry), so you're going to have deal with it sooner or later. Why not now?

11-20: Wow! You're very well adjusted. I've never met you, but I would certainly like to. If you're a single woman close to my age (okay, any age), track me down and we'll go out to dinner. Unfortunately, if you have the skills necessary to track me down, you're probably just my next stalker, not my eternal companion. Oh well.

21-30:   You're making progress and you should be proud of yourself. It takes time to overcome the emotional trauma of divorce, but you're on your way. Don't be afraid to seek out a qualified therapist to help you through this. If you start dating the therapist, however, you both have problems beyond the scope of this BS scale, which should be addressed by a professional therapist. No, wait. Try heavy medication this time.

31-39:   Be afraid. Be very afraid. No, I'm not talking to you. I'm talking to all your friends and relatives. You're driving them insane, and there's no end in sight. If you're not already paranoid, you should be because they're plotting behind your back to have you hospitalized, or at least heavily medicated. Watch out for Marlin Perkins look-alikes "hanging out" on street corners with tranquilizer guns. Come to think of it, if you scored in the high 30's, perhaps you should listen to your friends instead of the voices in your head.

40 or higher: Go to the police and turn yourself in.

Meeting People –
The Cold, Hard, Mathematical Truth

"Do you believe that there's one person you're meant to be with, or do you think that it doesn't matter who you marry as long as you put forth the effort to make it work?"

I had been riding in the car, talking with Holly for about twenty minutes. We were on our way to Zion National Park, and the question was part of a general discussion on relationships. Holly and I had been dating for four months and were continually amazed at how compatible we were. The only hitch in our relationship was the 500 miles that separated our homes, jobs, families, and lives. Other than that, it was a perfect match.

"Well," I started, "it seems to me that you could make a relationship work with any number of people. There are probably very few with whom you click on every level – very few where you really feel a magical connection. I dated for three years before I met you, and you're the first one that I've really connected with on every level. I'm thinking that by the time you sort through the 300 million people in the United States, and find a nice, single, temple-worthy, LDS girl with a sense of humor, whom I find physically attractive, intellectually stimulating, emotionally stable, and spiritually

sound, and who is attracted to me, there are probably 300 women that I would match with as well as I do you."

"So," I continued, smiling, "I guess that makes you one-in-a-million."

She laughed. "Now all you have to do is find the one that lives in your area code."

Random Encounters

I'll grant you that the statistics of being single can be discouraging at times. Let's do a little quick math and see what we come up with. Because I'm living in America, I'm going to base my calculations on the 300 million people living here in the United States.

According to the church statistical report presented at the April, 2005 general conference, there are 12,275,822 members of the church worldwide. I'm looking for one that's single, female, active in church, within 130 miles of Las Vegas (my hometown), within a few years of my age, heterosexual, and holds a temple recommend, whom I find physically attractive, emotionally stable, intellectually stimulating, and spiritually uplifting, and who feels the same way about me. Let's run the numbers.

12,275,822	members
x 20 %	single
x 50 %	female
x 50 %	active in the church
x 1.57 %	within 130 miles of my house
x 15 %	close to my age
x 99.97 %	heterosexual
x 30 %	holds temple recommend
x 30 %	physically, my type
x 20 %	emotionally stable
x 48 %	intellectually stimulating
x 38 %	spiritually uplifting
x 20 %	likes me

What I have found with this model is that there is nearly an entire person (0.949) who meets my rather reasonable requirements. For the record, fractional people are either very slender or completely comatose. All is not lost, however. By compromising on one category or another, I raise my odds of finding someone. For example, if it's not important that someone likes me, there are 4.745 people that fit the bill. With nearly five people out there who are perfect for me, but will find me annoying and childish, I can't help but be optimistic. Every time I meet someone new there is a 0.0000016 % chance that I'll almost find happiness.

If you're willing to travel, your odds increase dramatically. If I remove the geographic requirement, there are 298 women out there who are perfect for me, and vice-versa. That's not even counting the fractional hottie (she's only 0.3 in this calculation, so I'm worried about her). Half are in the United States, so my eternal companion (wherever she is) is actually one in two million, not one in a million.

Have some fun, and do a little math of your own. You might not be looking for the person I've described in this mathematical model, so feel free to drop your own specifications into the equation and re-calculate. If something is negotiable to you, such as geography, emotional stability, or sexual orientation, the statistical probability of finding someone special may rise to 1 in 900,000 or even 1 in 850,000. Don't you just love math?

The point of this exercise is not to discourage you with the impossible odds of finding that someone special. The point is that it will take a miracle, so you need the Lord's help. Also, you can't sit around and wait for a random encounter. You have to take matters into your own hands (and pray a lot for that miracle). Fortunately, there are a number of ways to increase your odds of meeting someone compatible, including church-sponsored single events, blind dates, and the internet.

Church-Sponsored Singles Events

If you are LDS and single, you are in one of two groups. Either you are 18-30 years of age, or you are older. I began my career as a SAM (Single Again Mormon) in the 18-30 category and attended a number of church-sponsored functions in an attempt to widen my social circle from just me to me and anybody else. Sounds easy and risk-free, doesn't it? So does making miniature cakes in a little plastic oven heated by a light bulb, but several local firemen and I can attest otherwise.

I recall one such event, Family Home Evening. I'm certain it was Family Home Evening because the gym was filled with lunatics, "lunatics" comes from the same Latin root as Lunes, which is the Spanish word for Monday, and Family Home Evening is always on Monday night (don't try this at home, I've been using pneumonic memory devices for many years).

On this particular evening, the ward was playing dodgeball in the gym. I knew this because periodically, a young lady would emerge from the gym holding her hand to her nose in a futile attempt to stem the flow of blood. Usually a couple of Relief Society sisters accompanied her shouting helpful suggestions such as, "Gross," and "It looks broken." Occasionally a young man would be trailing and spouting off apologies as fast as possible, stopping only to wince when she turned and exposed the bruised and bloody mess that had been her face before he had introduced it to a rubber playground ball at 95 miles per hour.

When I arrived at this officially sanctioned mayhem, I didn't get any further than the foyer. That's because there was an attractive young woman sitting in a chair screaming with her very closed body language that she did not want to be disturbed. She seemed to be critiquing the masonry work on the far wall, concentrating so hard on one particular brick that I fully expected it to break loose and fly across the room.

Approaching her in the suave, sophisticated manner with which I am cursed and which I simply cannot turn off, I hit her with one of my suave and sophisticated opening lines. "So whatcha lookin' at?"

As her gaze turned from the wall to me, her expression did not change, and I could feel the anger rays from her eyes boring through my skull. Uh oh. What had I done?

"I was just noticing all of the flaws in that wall." The rays intensified, but I simply ignored the fact that her anger had turned from the wall to me. She was quite obviously a bitter, angry woman, and that was my specialty. (I want to clarify that I no longer specialize in bitter, angry women. In fact, I generally refer them out to other guys. For a time, however, my strategy for meeting women revolved around the fact that bitter, angry women are looking for someone to focus their hatred on, and I was craving attention. Any parent will tell you that sometimes kids will do whatever it takes to get attention, negative or positive. I had found that bitter, angry women are happy to give you attention. It's in the form of violent diatribes against men in general and you in particular, but it's attention. Of course, I didn't realize this at the time. That's how my therapist explained it to me later.)

But I digress. Drawing upon my observational and deductive reasoning skills, I cleverly noted, "I'm guessing you're just here so you can tell your mother that you're trying."

A cold, hard chuckle emanated from her lips. "Actually, that's exactly why I'm here. The bonus is that from where I'm sitting, I get to see all the bloody noses on their way to the bathroom." Her lips split into a smile that sent shivers down my spine. Wow. She was a tough one. Time to lay on the charm.

"So would you rather stare at the wall or go get some ice cream?"

"If I leave for ice cream, who will critique the wall?"

"The wall will still be here on Sunday, but the ice cream will have melted by then."

She almost smiled, and we went out for ice cream, dated for 30 days, and moved on. This is how dating in young singles wards starts. Meet someone at an event, banter, go out a few times, and move on when they want to show you their knife, gun, or pepper spray collection. I met my schizophrenic stalker at Family Home Evening in much the same way. While it involved much hardship, attorneys, and a restraining order, the experience did help me get over my fascination with bitter, angry, and even "quirky" women. These are now red flags, not green lights.

While we're on the subject of young singles, you should be aware that telling someone you are divorced and mentioning that you have children are major bombshells for this age group. I recommend dropping them early and watching closely for a reaction. If you're dating someone younger than 30, expect a shock. Interestingly, these bombs lose some force as you and your dates age. Once they cross the age barrier, divorce and children are anticipated and even expected. While there are some exceptions, I stand by this as a general rule.

After a short time in the young singles group, I graduated into the "mature" single adult program, which I refer to as the "31 until death takes us" age group. Like many new members of this age group, I did not jump at the chance to attend dances, parties, and game nights right away.

One evening, shortly after turning 31, I had a very sobering experience. My father is a nice, single guy who looks much younger than his actual age of approximately 900 years (remember, that's an approximation). He has a few quirks of his own and has been actively inactive in the church since approximately the time of my birth. He approached me just when I was thinking about going to a dance and said, "Did you know that the church has dances for **our** age group every weekend? You should come. We always have a great time."

That single statement, made by a loving parent trying to encourage his son to greater social interaction, kept me from attending a dance for over three years. I have since attended a number of dances for "mature" LDS singles, and by a number I mean the number two. During those two dances, however, I sought to confirm hypotheses formed through a series of interviews with individuals who regularly attend such gatherings.

First, there seems to be a core of individuals who attend all of the dances, firesides, and game nights simply because they enjoy them. We'll call them regulars. Having already dated all the other regulars of the appropriate gender and age, they are realistic about the odds of actually meeting their eternal companion at these events, and are able to simply enjoy themselves because they've given up all hope.

Next, there are those who come and sit in their car in the parking lot, watching to see who else goes in. In this example, let's say a woman is skulking behind her steering wheel on the far side of the parking lot. If she sees someone she would like to meet, or if her inner dialogue is convincing enough ("Come on. You can do this. Don't be afraid. Just go in for five minutes. It won't kill you. Maybe you'll meet someone nice. It's Friday night. You can't spend every weekend alone with a pint of pistachio ice cream. Now get out of the car and get in there."), she'll go inside.

Once inside, this brave woman will immediately wish she was in her car on the way to the store for a pint of pistachio ice cream. Looking around, she will not see a single man whom she finds remotely attractive. She will, however, see several men of some generation other than her own making a beeline across the dance floor toward her. At this point she will flee. Shortly after her departure, several attractive men her age will emerge from the restroom, see that there are still no women of their generation in attendance and leave in disgust.

Thus you will find that if you are a thirty-something man, there are no women your age at the dance because the old men have chased them all away. If you are a thirty-something woman, you will be frightened to attend because of all the old men and because there are no guys your age at the dances anyway. If you're an older man, you're insulted at the rudeness of the younger women whom you try to meet and discouraged by their physical conditioning (they can run very fast). And, of course, all the older women are disgusted by the behavior of the men their age and refuse to attend rather than continue to witness such an inappropriate display. Thus, only those who have no hope or expectation of meeting anyone attend these dances – the regulars.

I think what we've discovered is that we can fix the system if we simply don't allow any old men to attend the dances. Okay, that is patently unfair. We allow them to attend, but all men over sixty will be required to wear shock collars that produce a jolt of electricity if they wander within ten feet of a woman under forty. It may seem cruel, but it's better than exposing them to the emotional pain resulting from flat-out rejection or a potential heart attack brought on by the exertion of chasing younger women out the door and across the parking lot as they try to get a phone number. While this is obviously for the greater good, I reserve the right to change my opinion as I continue to age. I'm certain that I won't find this funny at all in a few years.

As you attend these events, you may want to start a database of people you meet. I know a woman who dated over two hundred men in a six month period. She had names, photos, descriptions, and interesting facts listed for each one. She also kept track of what she had worn and where she had gone on dates with each of them in order to keep her confusion to a minimum. Say what you will, but such a system helps avoid the ever-present danger of introducing yourself and getting the following response: "Yeah, I know. We went out to dinner last year. Remember?"

Blind Dates

At some point, your friends and family will try to set you up on a blind date. They will express their desire to help you find your eternal companion, that special someone with whom you share a magical connection. They will assure you that they know someone who is absolutely perfect for you: intelligent, sensitive, kind, spiritual, and good looking.

They're lying.

I don't mean to imply that your loved ones would lie to you, but they are lying to you. Okay, I will grant you that it might not be an intentional lie, but there are, nonetheless, a number of untruths flying around.

Here's how this well-intentioned tragedy unfolds. Someone who cares about you and wants to fill the void that they see in your life (let's say your sister for the purposes of this example) decides to keep an eye out for eligible companions for you. Her fixation on finding someone that's single leads her to overlook all other compatibility issues (this stage of the blind date trap can be particularly hazardous if your sister happens to work at the public defender's office, the state unemployment center, or Radio Shack).

Her burning desire clouds her judgment to the point that when she meets an alcoholic, one-eyed prostitute being charged with manslaughter in connection with a previous relationship (or even worse – an attorney), she immediately says, "You're single? So is my brother. You would be perfect for each other. I'll set it up." Of course, this is assuming you're not into alcoholic, one-eyed prostitutes being charged with manslaughter (or attorneys). If you are, I offer my apologies. I'm sure you'll be very happy together (editor's note: this was in no way intended to be a slight against all the alcoholic, one-eyed prostitutes being charged with manslaughter out there).

So you allow your sister to set you up on a blind date. Because you're too smart to let this random person know where you live, you meet at a restaurant. At this point, all you know about your date is that she is really, really sweet, and your sister cannot fathom how she is still single.

During dinner you will discover one of several

things. One possibility is that your dinner companion does not have a firm enough grasp on the English language to distinguish between the term "blind date" and the term "therapy session." If she starts telling you anything about her ex-husband, family dysfunctions, or Amway, this is an indication that you should be charging counseling fees for the conversation rather than paying for dinner. Try to subtly redirect the conversation with phrases like: Your face gets all pudgy when you talk, I don't care about that, or blah, blah, blah, wah, wah, wah. Don't forget body language. Long exasperated sighs, rolling your eyes, and sliding slowly off your chair to the floor can all relate your painfully intense boredom and disinterest.

Another common blind date discovery is that your new friend has the social skills of a toddler, so you are embarrassed by them and for them, both publicly and privately. Examples include: showing you his collection of Star Wars action figures (not dolls) before you go out; asking you to bless the food at a nice restaurant, and angrily shushing people at the surrounding tables for increased reverence; or putting a Weird Al Yankovic CD in the car stereo, singing along loudly (and poorly), and glaring at you when you begin singing in an effort to reduce the awkwardness of the moment. I wish that I could say that these are fictional examples. Unfortunately, they are all part of a single date, related to me by a friend who has an uncanny ability to attract men with the social skills of a dromedary after it's been in the desert for three months (and you know how much worse they are than regular camels).

You may find yourself on a blind date with someone who has no personality, or someone with way, way too much personality – both of which are equally painful. It's hard to say whether it's tougher to drag a conversation out of someone intent on answering all your conversation starters with yes or no, or trying to get a word in with someone who seems to be part dolphin because they only have to take a breath every fifteen minutes. Either way you will be exhausted by the end of the date.

You don't have to feel trapped though. Pass the time by playing a little game. If you're with Mr. No Personality see how long you can drag out the silence. Reward yourself with dessert if you can go more than twenty minutes. If your date won't stop talking, keep track of the number of first person, personal pronouns (I, me, my, and mine) that come out of his mouth during every ten minute period. Keep score on your napkin. Anything over fifty should be considered an Olympic-type effort, and may indicate that you're dating an actual celebrity, a woman with an inflated ego, or an average guy.

If you sense that your date is a habitual liar, or simply likes to exaggerate his accomplishments, push him for details on his stories. It should prove entertaining, and every once in a while you can find someone who climbed Mount Everest, orbited the Earth, solved a Rubik's Cube, or does his home teaching on the first of every month.

Another common blind date discovery is that your new friend carries an engagement ring with him everywhere he goes, just in case you happen to be "the one." By the time the entrée arrives, he's had a profound revelatory experience and is working up his courage to propose. And he will find the courage to propose to you on your blind date. It's not like he hasn't had plenty of practice. He gets manifestations like this all the time. He's full of something, but it's not the Spirit.

If you find yourself in one of these tragically common situations, don't worry. There are a number of quick and easy ways to get out of your date early without creating undue embarrassment for you or your companion. The most obvious is to fake a grand mal seizure. This way you don't have to get up and walk out of a crowded restaurant in the middle of a meal. The paramedics will take you out on a stretcher. Once you reach the ambulance, you're free and clear because only family members can ride in the ambulance with you. Just ask the paramedics to drop you off at home. They're used to this, but a tip is considered customary. If you're lucky, one of the paramedics will be cute, so the evening won't be a total loss.

Another classy way out of a bad situation is to start a small fire. Once the smoke alarms and sprinklers go off, it's easy to become separated in the confusion. You'll have to be prepared to cover the costs of smoke and fire damage, but it might be worth it to avoid, "I brought along my old wedding photos so we could reminisce about the life I used to have that I'm completely over and have moved past and am not at all bitter or emotional about any more."

If subtlety is not important to you, simply run screaming from the room. Be certain, however, to take your purse, glasses, and jacket with you because it's really embarrassing and theatrically anticlimactic to have to skulk back to the table to retrieve them after such a dramatic exit. Also, you should leave a dollar on the table because I know that if I had a dollar for every time someone ran screaming from my table, I'd be a rich man today.

Once you return home from your blind date, you will be expected to report to your sister who arranged the meeting. She has been waiting with great anticipation to hear how you think this might be the one. As you relate tales of arguments with waiters, psychotic episodes at movies, rants about political issues, and how she (or worse, he) has a very small dog that she treats like a person, your well-meaning sibling will be on the floor, overcome with laughter and quite possibly needing an oxygen tank to recover. Do not provide one.

At this point, you're really in trouble because now you've changed your sister's motivation. She might have started out wanting to help you find your eternal companion, but now that she sees how entertaining the train wreck you call dating can be, she's looking for the most entertaining story possible. That means if you continue to trust your sister, there is nothing but cross-dressers, socially-challenged science fiction fans, and attorneys in your future. It's time to move beyond blind dates and take matters into your own hands.

Bonus Blind Date Tip: When someone asks, "Would you like to see the photos of my surgery?" the answer is always no.

The Internet

We've already discussed the horrors of blind dates, the statistical significance against random encounters, and the pre-pubescent awkwardness tied like an anchor to singles events. What's next?

So your life has reached a point where you thought, "Hey, maybe it would be a good idea to post my photograph and personal information on the internet in hopes that someone wonderful will spot me and want to contact me. Sure, there's a chance that I might end up needing to file for multiple restraining orders, but at this point I think it's worth the risk."

If you could hear yourself talking, you would be as horrified as I am right now. What has brought you to this point? For me, I had been meeting schizophrenic stalkers at Family Home Evening, and figured that the internet could not be much worse. An interesting theory. Let's examine the process.

For those who are new to dating, this is a great way to get your feet wet. Just go to www.lds(insert euphemism here).com. You don't have to post a photograph or any information until you're ready to interact with others. It's like catalog shopping. You can just look around at the other people who are online to see what's available. If you see something you like, you can think about it for a while before placing your order. Unfortunately, like catalog shopping, sometimes the photograph and description don't reflect the actual product as much as you had hoped, and the more popular items are often out of stock. Most items are refurbished, having been returned as damaged merchandise by someone else. All orders are COD, however, so if you change your mind you can always refuse delivery.

When you're ready to buy, you will have to place yourself on the auction block as well. This might seem a bit daunting, but don't worry, it's easier to be rejected relatively anonymously online than it is in person. To start, simply upload your photograph and write a profile that captures your character, personality, hopes, fears, dreams, strengths, and quirks in 300-500 words. As a professional writer, I hope I can give you some comfort by telling you that this is the most difficult writing exercise you will ever face. If you can put out of your mind the fact that thousands of strangers (and potential relationship partners) will be judging you and your relative mental health by the words you assemble in this section, you probably won't embarrass yourself too badly. Of course, they'll never even read your profile if they don't like your picture, but try not to think about that too much either – it could make you a little self-conscious.

While we're on photos, make sure you post one that reflects what you really look like. It's bad when no one responds to your photo because you just don't photograph well. It's worse when you get a ton of responses because you're really good with Photoshop. One day you'll have to meet some of these people, and you don't want them to feel shocked and betrayed when they see you for the first time.

Now you're shopping and available for review by other shoppers. When you see something you like, you need to send a message. Don't bother sending the flirt, wink, or smile – those little canned messages provided by the catalog for those who get tongue tied even via email. These are the equivalent of waving to someone in traffic and will get the same results. I recommend a few straightforward questions asking for details on their education or career. If you try to be clever and funny, you will occasionally find someone who appreciates your sense of humor, but more often you will be shunned because it's hard to tell the difference between funny and psycho in an introductory email.

If they respond to your message, congratulations! Now you've got a dialogue and can try to get to know someone new at an easy pace. Between their profile, a few emails, and a couple phone calls, you should get a pretty good read on the other person's personality, mental health, and criminal record. Trust your instincts.

If they don't respond, that's okay. One of the advantages of the internet is that it's impersonal and relatively anonymous. Go with it. There's no point in getting mad at someone for not responding. If you think they're attractive, 10,000 other people probably do also, and they get more messages than they can possibly respond to (as, I'm sure, do you).

If you get an email from someone, and you're not sure if you want to respond, use this handy guide to help you:

- Do you find them physically attractive?
- Does their profile represent the type of person whom you could respect for their spiritual, emotional, and intellectual strengths?
- Does Moroni descend from the heavens in a pillar of light to bring peace to your soul and assurance that your new online buddy is a good person?
- If you're still a little uncertain after Moroni's visit, does the background check you ordered support the angel's proclamation from the heavens?

If you answered "yes" to all of the above, it's probably safe to respond with some questions of your own. I recommend subtle queries that gently get at the real questions on your mind without being offensive.

What you want to ask	Acceptable Alternative
Are you in shape?	How often do you work out?
Do you have a job?	Do you enjoy your work?
Do you have a job?	What's a typical day like for you?
Do you have a job?	How long is your daily commute?
Are you educated?	Where did you go to school?
Are you a redneck?	What kind of music do you like?
How much money do you make?	Where do you live? Do you like to travel?
How's your personal hygiene?	How long does it take you to get ready in the morning?
Are you nuts?	So what do you think about... (pick any controversial subject)?
Are you bitter and angry?	What was your last boyfriend like?
Are you willing to move?	Do you like where you live?

After you've exchanged a few emails, you'll have to make a decision. Do you escalate your communication from written to verbal, or do you stop it right here? Again, if you're not comfortable taking the next step, the easy way out is to simply stop writing. It's okay. Everyone is annoyed the first few times someone stops responding to their emails, but they soon learn that it's widely accepted as the best way to avoid long, involved conversations about why you shouldn't pursue a relationship that doesn't really exist.

Warning: By putting your photo and personal information on the internet, you're setting yourself up for some awkward moments. I was recently cornered at a fireside by someone who seemed to know me. Eventually, I discovered that I wasn't a moron who had forgotten this woman and the time we spent together (although that can happen). In fact, we had never met. She simply recognized me from an online website and a couple of emails the previous year. If it wasn't a little bit scary, it would have been really funny.

Anyway, once you've established verbal communication, it's just like being set up on a blind date. If you find him charming and captivating, set a time to meet him in a public place, pay your tithing and insurance, and pray that this will at least be the source of a funny story that you share with your single friends, not your therapist.

Dating... Again

So you've run out of those little hairs on your arm to pull out on Friday nights, and you're looking for a new way to introduce pain into your life? You're in luck because you're now eligible for that interpersonal game of Russian Roulette known as dating.

Initial Meeting and Evaluation

Don't think of dating as some sort of competition where you're judged, ranked against every other member of your gender, and cast off if you don't measure up – think of it as a series of competitions where you're continually judged, ranked against every other member of your gender, and cast off if you don't measure up. That's right. Not only do you get to be silently critiqued by the same person over a number of dates, you get to repeat the process with every single person you meet. Now before that fetal position becomes so tight that you can't get your sobs out, keep in mind that you'll soon learn to be shallow and judgmental of them as well.

I think once you understand the process, you

won't be so self-conscious about dating. So let's go through it step by step. First, you meet someone. If you're a woman, then the size and shape of your legs, butt, stomach, and breasts have been analyzed and rated within the first 0.0042 seconds. If you pass that lengthy, in-depth evaluation, the man shaking your hand will look at your face. If he likes what he sees (and again, don't feel self-conscious about this), he will talk to you with intense interest, wanting to know your name, number, vital stats, life story, favorite dessert, hopes, fears, dreams, etc. If not, you will notice him glancing at someone else for 0.0042 seconds. I don't know how, but women can detect a break in eye contact that lasts less time than it takes a hummingbird to flap its wings.

If you're a man meeting someone new, you won't notice any evaluating looks. This is because you've already been judged by several of the woman's friends who put together a nice report with color graphs, charts, digitally-produced images of what you will look like in ten years, and pro formas on your future earnings. If the reports were negative or she doesn't like what she sees, the woman will maintain a casual disinterest while she engages in polite conversation with you. If the reports were positive and she really likes the way you look, she will maintain a casual disinterest while she engages in polite conversation with you. So how do you tell the difference? If she's surrounded by friends, you haven't made it past the physical evaluation. If you're having a one-on-one conversation, congratulations.

Getting to Know You

Let's assume that you have both passed the test of physical attraction. Next comes conversation. You and your opponent are now fencing to determine if there is intellectual, emotional, and spiritual compatibility on a superficial level. Refer to the table in the online dating section to find polite ways to ask important questions about education, employment, hygiene, emotional stability, etc.

You must be very careful. This is when it's most tempting to lie. If you feel that you're losing the fencing match, you may inadvertently blurt out something that isn't true, such as, "I played football for the Denver Broncos," "I'm a brain surgeon," or "That's hair gel, not head lice." Eventually, these little white lies will come back to haunt you. Good luck explaining why a brain surgeon drives a Volkswagen, or why you don't travel with the team.

There's really no sense in lying or even exaggerating because eventually the truth will come out. She will find out that you don't "technically" have a temple recommend, and he will discover that you're not really a huge basketball fan (like when you ask if the yellow team just got a first down). Then the relationship will end because you've lied and broken the fragile trust that's so important. It's better to be honest from the beginning, so that the relationship never gets started in the first place.

Unfortunately, there are still some who will bend the truth a little ("little" being a relative term). Sometimes it's so subtle that those speaking don't even consider it lying.

Still, it's nice to be able to glean the truth from these little, white lies, so I've included this handy interpretation guide.

What they say	What they mean
I'm helping my mother out.	I live with my parents.
I'm self-employed; I own my own business; I'm an entrepreneur; I'm between jobs.	I'm unemployed.
I really, really love exercising.	I hate exercising.
I never watch television.	I'm a couch potato.
I love camping and hiking.	I went hiking once.
I don't mind long-distance relationships.	I'm afraid of commitment.
I feel this strange connection to you.	I'm desperate.
Where do you see this relationship going?	I'm desperate.
I don't want to rush anything, but…	I'm desperate.
I've never told anyone this before.	I try this on everyone.
It's like Rush Limbaugh always says…	I'm psycho.
I had a great time. I'll call you sometime.	I don't like you. Don't call me.

What they say	What they mean
I'm looking at new cars right now.	I can get another 40,000 miles out of this hunk of junk.
That's really interesting.	You're really cute, and I want to make out with you.
Well, have a nice week.	I won't call or see you for the rest of the week.
Let's meet at the temple.	I want to know if you really have a temple recommend, or if you're lying like all the others.
My ex and I have some communication problems.	We hate each other and act like five-year-olds when we're in the same room.
I think you are the greatest guy...	I'm about to break up with you
I would be so lucky to marry you...	But that's never going to happen because I'm about to break up with you.
... but I still want to be friends.	I mean the kind of friends that don't call each other or do things together or make eye contact if they end up passing in the hallway sometime.

While you're dating, keep an eye out for red flags that might indicate little white lies, such as federal agents making inquiries as to his whereabouts. I know a girl who discovered, almost too late, that her fiancé wasn't "technically" a medical doctor in the sense that he hadn't actually gone to medical school, passed medical exams, or been licensed by the medical board. When the feds informed her of this, his little white lie ("I'm a doctor") drove a wedge into their relationship that was pounded home by a thoughtless judge "protecting the public's safety." And yes, his patients were a little upset too.

Can you see how this might have started? This guy, wanting to impress a girl he's dating, tells her that he's in medical school. They date for a couple years. She naturally expects him to graduate and practice medicine, so he has to set up an office, see patients, and maybe even perform some unnecessary surgery just to keep up this little white lie he told to impress a girl. He could come clean, but, come on, that would be really embarrassing. In the end, the only one not hurt by his lie was his new roommate (okay, cellmate), Bubba.

Rebounding

If you go out with someone who has recently ended a serious relationship, they are on the rebound. If you're looking for a shallow, physical, short-term relationship, or a twisted, codependent relationship that could last forever, by all means, seek these people out.

Generally, however, you will want to avoid these people as you would avoid other mildly disturbing occurrences, such as IRS audits, rabies from wild animal bites in embarrassing locations (excluding rabid wolverines on your head), and biblical plagues (frogs, flies, locusts, etc.).

Fortunately, I've developed a short quiz to help you determine if you've met someone who is on the rebound.

1. Does she weep for no apparent reason?
2. Does he keep calling you by the wrong name?
3. Have her internal monologues become external? Mumbling is a key indicator of this.
4. Does he compare you to his last girlfriend, positively or negatively (e.g. You are so much nicer than Janice)?
5. Does he cut sentences short when waxing nostalgic (e.g. I used to come here all the time with… well, never mind)?
6. Do subtle, yet bitter, accusations come from nowhere (e.g. Sorry. I forgot that **some** guys don't like to hold hands in public)?
7. Does he ask for relationship advice or insight into your gender's way of thinking while he's hitting on you?

If you can answer affirmatively to two or more of the questions above, gently explain to your new friend that you don't think he's ready to start dating again. Or simply excuse yourself to use the restroom, climb out a window, crawl on your stomach to your vehicle, and don't spare the rubber or the horses on your way out of the parking lot. It's your call.

The Dating Game

If dating isn't fun, then why do they call it the dating game? Ironically, everybody wants to have a good time, but nobody wants to "play games." Ask any single person, and they will assure you that they detest playing games. They never play games themselves, and they certainly don't want to go out with other people that play games.

They are lying. Oh, I don't think it's an intentional lie. It's more like when someone says that they want to surf a tidal wave, experience a forest fire up close, or swim with the sharks. They may think they want those things, but they have no comprehension of the horrible forces to which they would be exposing themselves in the same way that a moth has no concept of the power of electricity as it works its way towards the beckoning, luminescent center of a bug zapper.

Everyone plays the game. If you refuse to play, you simply forfeit, and that's no way to make the playoffs. Perhaps it would help if I explained the rules. Keep in mind that the rules vary by state, region, and individual.

Many people think that the game is about pretending not to care about someone (so they'll find you more desirable), making out without commitment, or hurting people's feelings just for the fun of it. While you'll run into a few people (90%) that have this approach, the game in its pure form is really about getting to know someone at a comfortable pace.

For example, let's say that Gary and Mary go out on a first date and have a great time. Gary tells Mary that he had a good time and asks if she would like to go out again. Mary's response will dictate the rules of the game to follow. I've included a series of handy charts below to help you follow along.

Chart #1

Mary's Response	Meaning / Result
Mary smiles, uses the word sometime, and starts talking about how busy her schedule is.	Mary doesn't want to play. She doesn't like Gary enough to go out on another date. Game over – Gary loses.
Mary reciprocates by saying that she had a good time too.	The game is on. Gary has no idea if she means it or if she's just being polite. Go to chart #2.
Mary says she had a great time, and tries to set a specific date and time for their next outing.	She's playing, but she's starting out with slow pitch softball. Maybe she's honest and genuine, but maybe she's setting him up. Go to chart #3.
Mary tells Gary that she really likes him and wants to spend a lot of time getting to know him.	Gary will not call. Game over – Mary loses. Unless she was only bluffing and really wanted to get rid of him without making a scene. Then she gets a secret victory.

Chart #2

Gary's Response	Meaning / Result
Gary says he'll give her a call sometime to set up the date.	Gary has taken control and is firmly in the driver's seat. By all accounts he is now winning the game. Go to chart #4
Gary tries to set up a specific date and time for their next date.	A risky move, especially because she avoided the question earlier. He's showing a lot of trust or naiveté by exposing himself to immediate rejection. Go to chart #5.
Gary does not press the issue. Neither person calls or follows up for fear of putting the other party in a position of control.	Game over – Draw. Both Gary and Mary are losers.

Chart #3

Gary's Response	Meaning / Result
They set the details for their next date.	Push – Move on to round two.
Gary hedges, and says he'll call her later to set the details.	Gary is winning because the ball is in his court, and Mary has exposed herself (figuratively).
Gary tries to set a date for the following day or tries to line up two dates at once.	Mary is winning because Gary overreached and is no longer in control and "hard to get." He just looks desperate.

Chart #4

Gary's Move	Meaning / Result
Gary calls Mary later that day to set up another date.	Gary Loses. If Mary did want to go out again, she changes her mind when he comes on too strong and scares her away.
Gary calls Mary the next day to set up another date.	Mary is winning. She can use her advantage to slam dunk Gary, or she can play nice.
Gary calls Mary after two days to set up another date.	The game is tied, and the ball is in Mary's court.
Gary calls Mary after six days to set up another date.	Gary loses. He waited too long and Mary's interest has been replaced by bitterness and anger (or redirected to a blind date arranged by her sister). This could be spectacular.

Chart #5

Mary's Response	Meaning / Result
Mary balks on setting details for the next date.	Mary's winning. In fact, she has already won (she's not going out with Gary again). Now she's just trying to stretch out the pain, so she can bask in the glow of her victory.
Mary sets details for the next date.	Push – Move on to round two.
Mary tries to set a date for later in the same week.	Gary's winning. He can agree for a push, or he can force it to next week to give himself the upper hand.

As you can see, the game is really pretty straightforward. If you don't like playing the game and end up on a date with someone who feels the same way, you can play nice. I must repeat my earlier warning though. If you and your date strive to be open and honest rather than trying to manipulate each other, you might end up with a solid relationship built on trust and respect. Don't say I didn't warn you.

Even if you're able to take this rare option, don't fool yourselves. You're still playing the game. You're just playing nicely. This is because if you share all of your feelings with someone you don't know very well, their response will be to run screaming from the room. If this is not their response, there is something seriously wrong with them, and you should run screaming from the room.

Just because you have a deeply spiritual experience by which you know that they are the one for you (and also which horse will win the Kentucky Derby), does not mean that you should share this information with them right away. You should call your bookie first. No, really. You can't show all your cards immediately because you just don't know how they'll respond to such an information overload. Save it for the second date.

First Date

Okay, you've met someone, you know about the game, and you've successfully set up a date. You'll want to meet your date at a restaurant or other public place. In today's society, the guy does not pick up the girl at her home for the first date because the girl already has restraining orders out against her last three dates and still wishes that her ex-husband didn't know where she lived. Safety first.

Remember, she might be psycho too, so you don't want to share any personal information (such as your name) that would allow her to find you later if you don't want to be found. In fact, I recommend meeting at a restaurant you don't particularly enjoy. That way it's not a sacrifice when you can't go back because she's camped out in the parking lot hoping to pick up your trail, so she can follow you to work and surprise you during your big presentation.

Dinner is out of the question for a first date. There are too many unknowns: how long do we linger at the table when we're done eating, are we doing something after dinner, is it safe to get in his car if we do decide to do something, what time does the date end, is that spinach stuck in her teeth, and do we end the evening with a kiss? Plan a mid-week lunch instead. Most people have one hour away from work for lunch. There is a clock ticking from the moment you meet at the restaurant. And you don't have to make a point of saying, "People know where I am and will worry if I'm not back on time." It's assumed.

If the date goes well, you both leave wanting more. If not, you only have to endure their presence for an hour, tops. Plus, since nobody kisses at lunchtime, there's no need to order the garlic bread in order to avoid an awkward pause when you say goodbye.

Okay, you're at lunch and you've begun the verbal sparring (getting-to-know-you) phase of the date. What you're doing here is walking a tightrope – balance is the key. If you're not balanced, you will fall into The Chasm below (often referred to as The Gulf of Misery and Endless Woe). You need to impress the other person enough that they will want to learn more about you. You can't appear as if you're trying to impress them, however, because that seems egotistical, self-centered, and worst of all, desperate.

Let's say, for example, that you have two Master's degrees, you publish a family magazine, you're a fifth degree black belt, and you complete your home teaching on the first of every month (okay, that last one is overdoing it, but you get the picture). You can't just come out and share all that information in the first ten minutes. You'll look like an insecure, arrogant braggart. Of course, women are so used to hearing this from guys that if you don't start bragging right away, they may assume you don't have any accomplishments. Guys, don't panic. She will probably start asking questions to see if you've done anything with your life. Of course, if you haven't done anything with your life, this can be a little awkward.

Remember, accomplishments should only be shared in response to direct questions, or if you're desperate and afraid you'll lose the chance to impress your date. The key is to steer the conversation towards those direct questions. You don't want to come right out and tell the story about the time you rescued Marie Osmond from shark-infested waters near an island in the Bahamas, which the locals renamed in your honor during an elaborate native ceremony to commemorate your heroic act. Instead, simply mention that you just returned from a lovely vacation on the beautiful island of Dave (insert your name here). "What?" you respond to her query. "Yes, that would be quite a coincidence, but there's actually an interesting story behind it. I'll have to tell you sometime. Now? Well, if you insist."

Now your heroism is surpassed only by your humility. What a guy.

If you're unable to steer the conversation around

how wonderful you are, you may have to pretend to be interested in the other person. If they are also faking sincere modesty or are simply boring, however, you're going to have to carry your end of the first date on the strength of your personality alone. If you don't have a personality, I recommend getting one. They come in handy in a wide variety of social situations. They practically pay for themselves in the first year alone. You can't order them online, but you can rehearse a given personality until it feels perfectly natural. Here are some of the more popular ones.

> **Workaholic** – Avoids close, interpersonal relationships through a driving need to succeed in business. If you choose this personality, you may be able to afford extravagant cars, homes, and nights out on the town, and you won't have to spend much time dating because you'll be "too busy." On the down side, you will be hit by a barrage of platitudes from your mother ranging from, "No one ever wished on his deathbed that he'd spent more time at the office," to "No success can compensate for failure in the home." You will hate your voicemail.

> **Fitness Fanatic** – The advantage of this personality is that you'll be in outstanding physical shape. The bad news is that you'll take fitness to such an extreme that no one will want to spend time with you once they get to know you. Be sure to tell everyone you meet what you have eaten during

the day (vegetables only), details on your workout routine (which should take at least three hours daily), and, most importantly, ways that they can get rid of their little problem areas. Being fit isn't enough. You must also be obsessive, neglecting all other areas of your life in order to really bring this personality to life.

Molly / Peter – To fill this stereotype properly, you must not only be sincere and humble, but you must be more sincere and humble than anyone else. It is vitally important that you are more humble, devoted, selfless, and non-competitive than anyone else. Take time to point out to others how they can increase their own spiritual growth. No need to wait until they ask for advice. They're probably too shy, and, frankly, intimidated by your overwhelming humility and greatness.

Exaggerator – Life's a stage, and you're the star. You're the strongest, fastest, and smartest. Your accomplishments make those of historic statesmen, generals, and scientists look like the bumblings of two of the three stooges. Exotic, amazing, and unverifiable, the stories of your adventures will keep listeners on the edge of their seat as you weave epic tales in which you are the hero who prevails over all that life has thrown at you. Indeed, you will remind your dates of another man whose life truly amazed and inspired millions, Forrest Gump.

PMESHBI (Physically, Mentally, Emotionally, and Spiritually Healthy and Balanced Individual)– Nice try. Much like Bigfoot, the Loch Ness Monster, and a minivan that makes you look cool, these individuals are rumored to exist, but a lack of confirmed sightings casts doubt on their reality. You can't fake this personality. If you try, everyone you go out with will pick you apart in an effort to prove that you don't really exist. You will be assigned the Exaggerator personality by default.

Bitter – Now this is more like it! If you're recently divorced, you won't have to stretch to find this personality. It's lying right beneath the surface. You simply need to give it a voice. Certainly, this is the most entertaining personality of those listed. No need for manners or trying to impress someone. Simply rant, rave, and let that negativity shine (see the Bitterness Scale for more ideas). Keep in mind that you will have only one date with any given person because they will run screaming from the room after a short time. It will be worth it though because, really, you can't buy that kind of entertainment. Take care to avoid dating other bitter people, though. Commiseration can create an attraction so strong that before you know it, you're in the midst of your second divorce.

Now that you've picked a personality, be sure to stick with it for the remainder of the relationship (or your natural life, whichever comes first). If you switch back and forth between personalities, you will be labeled, and rightly so, as "a freaking psycho." So make sure you're comfortable with your personality before you start dating someone new.

If the first date goes well, you'll be wanting another one. In fact, you will both know within the first five minutes if you want a second date. Hopefully, you both feel the same way. If you're having a good time, but you can't read your date's emotions, here are some simple ways to increase your odds of a getting a second date while still on the first date:

- Compliment her on a little detail of her appearance: "I like your fingernails / shoes / hair / earrings."
- Make lots of eye contact, and do not stare at any particular body part (theirs, yours, or anyone else's) for a noticeable period of time. And remember we learned in the Initial Meeting and Evaluation section that she can detect shifts in visual focus as short as 0.0042 seconds. If you get caught, just shrug and move on because there's no smooth way out of this situation. For example, if your date looks up and you're staring at the waitress, she's not going to buy, "I think she's way too skinny, don't you?" or "I wish I could get her

attention because we're down to only seventeen breadsticks."

- Don't mention how many more children you do or don't want to have.
- Don't flirt with anyone who is not specifically out on a date with you.
- Remember, confessions are for the second date.
- Keep the "quirky" behavior under control. Tourette's syndrome makes good first impressions unlikely.
- I don't care what it is you collect. Don't tell her about it, and don't show it to her (not even pictures).
- Regardless of how cool your operation was, don't tell her about it.
- Try not to mention that your ex has a personality that reminds people of Jack Nicholson's character in *The Shining*. Let them discover that on their own.
- Do NOT offer to show her any scars.
- Most importantly, be yourself. If you happen across the nearly one person in the universe who finds you attractive, eternal bliss will be yours, and all the previous rejections will seem like tiny pinpricks. Of course, three thousand pinpricks can do a little damage along the way, but it will be worth it.

If you want to see your date again and he doesn't want to see you, that's called rejection, and it's okay.

Don't be afraid of rejection. Embrace it. You need to be okay with rejection and always keep a sharp eye out for it. Sometimes rejection can be very subtle, and you don't want to miss it. When you try to keep dating someone after they've rejected you, well, that's just sad.

We'll cover rejection in more detail in the chapter on breaking up. However, I do want to spend a moment here discussing the specific type of rejection that can occur between the first and theoretical second date.

Suppose that at the end of your lunch date, you say you had a great time and would like to see her again. If she pulls out her planner and sets up the next date with you then and there, you're in good shape. If she tells you to pick her up at home, that's a major vote of confidence in your mental and emotional state. Feel flattered.

If she tells you to give her a call, and you already have what you know to be a working phone number for her, you are still in pretty good shape (let's say 80% chance of a second date). If she gives you her number for the first time, that drops your odds a little bit to about 70%. When you give her a call that night (risky – remember the game that you're both playing, even if you hate the game and don't want to be playing) or the next day after work (better) you'll know more. If she answers and you can't find a time that you're both available for another date, you're probably being rejected very gently. You can try again later, but it'll just hurt more if you drag it out.

If she doesn't answer the phone, leave a message.

You don't want to call several times to try to catch her at home – that's just going to frighten her. Your phone number listed 27 times on her caller ID isn't romantic, it's evidence for a restraining order. If the phone number turns out to belong to the local pizzeria, don't worry about it. Yes, you've been rejected, but because of a thoughtful little detail on her part, you can soothe the pain a little with a pepperoni and mushroom pizza. Don't be afraid to get the stuffed crust. You deserve it.

Back to the restaurant. After you ask for a second date, remember that any hesitation on her part bodes poorly for you. Every second of hesitation reflects a 20% reduction in your odds of a second date. Suppose she hems and haws for five seconds and then says, "Yeah. That would be great. Give me a call sometime and we'll go out dancing or something." Guess what? You have a 0% chance of a second date. The hesitation was too long. She is, ironically just trying to spare your feelings (or trying escape without creating an ugly scene). When she leaves, stay at the restaurant and order dessert so you have something to do while you dissect the date, moment by moment, in an attempt to figure exactly where you blew it, so you won't do it again. Honestly, this is a pointless exercise because the truth is that you just weren't right for each other, but feel free to torture yourself anyway. Eventually, you'll learn that it's no big deal and just move on.

Congratulations! You've just survived a first date. About one in three will lead to second dates, and one in ten will lead to relationships. These "relationships" will, gratefully, keep you from going out on more first dates for a while, but they are double-edged swords as we'll see in later chapters.

Long Distance Relationships, Dating Non-Members, and Spitting into the Wind

What do these three things have in common? Well, you've received sage wisdom regarding the folly of all three of these practices, yet most of us have to learn the hard way.

I'll let you learn about spitting into the wind on your own. As far as relationships over vast distances (greater than 130 miles) and relationships with non-members, let this be a warning. The best thing that can happen is that you meet someone with whom you share amazing physical, emotional, intellectual, and spiritual chemistry, and fall in love. The worst thing that can happen is that you meet someone with whom you share amazing physical, emotional, intellectual, and spiritual chemistry, and fall in love.

If you should happen to meet your "soul mate" and they fall into one of these categories, well, now you have a problem. Don't you? Of course you do. Let's suppose that you meet the man of your dreams (I'm talking specifically to the ladies here). He's tall, handsome, loving, employed (dare I say, well-to-do), independent (he doesn't live with his mother), mature (no public farting here), and thinks you are the most wonderful person to ever walk the earth.

Calm down. This is hypothetical.

Oops! He lives in Wisconsin and you live in California. No problem. You can just move to Wisconsin, and... What's that? You don't want to pick up your life, quit your job, pull the kids out of school, and move to a state that has an average winter temperature that you didn't realize existed outside of the deep freezer that's holding 40 gallons of ice cream and a year's supply of protein in your garage? That's okay. I'm sure he's more than willing to move his life across the country for you. No? Hmm... Now we have a problem.

While you may feel certain that your emails, long telephone conversations, and occasional chaperoned weekends together have allowed you to see deep into his spirit to discern the type of man with whom you've fallen in love, part of you (presumably the part that watches the news and balances the checkbook) realizes that you really don't know this guy very well. I mean, come on, Bin Laden probably seems like a nice guy in small doses. It's not until you live in the same compound with him, spending time watching TV with him in his cave, and noticing the way that he has people executed all the time that you get to know the real Osama.

The point is that it takes time to get to know someone. It takes longer if you don't live nearby because you never get past the honeymoon phase, which is the phase where women wear makeup and guys always shower.

If you want to speed up the process and see what he's really like, I recommend a well-validated psychological technique employed by women the world over. Pick a fight. It really doesn't matter what the argument is about. In fact, the more trivial, the better. Attack his method of putting dishes in the dishwasher in the same way you would attack an 18th century fur trader for clubbing baby seals.

Now you get to see the real man behind the façade. If he's a volcano of anger bubbling under a thin layer of "trying to impress you," the beast will be revealed, and you will have dodged that particular bullet. Of course, you have to be careful. If he turns out to be the wonderful, caring, hero you had hoped he was, you will have just ruined the best relationship of your life by going overboard. Let's face it. Some women don't know their own strength when it comes to picking fights. Now you have to convince Mr. Wonderful that you're not a raving, psychotic lunatic – not an easy task considering that many of his previous dates have been with actual asylum escapees. Try this: "I'm not crazy. I was just picking a fight with you to see if you were really as nice as you seem to be because if you had yelled then you wouldn't really be nice but you didn't so it's all okay and we can forget the whole thing." Uh-oh. Sounds crazy. Better just kiss him. That usually fixes the problem.

Now to address another common mistake – dating non-members. There are many kind and wonderful people in the world that simply don't happen to be LDS. If they were all bad people, it would be easy not to date and fall in love with them. But they aren't, so now you have yourself a problem, don't you?

Since you ignored everyone's advice and got

yourself into this situation, let's look at your options. You can try to be subtle. Send the missionaries through their neighborhood, so they can randomly tract into their house. In this fantasy, your girlfriend invites the sister missionaries in to teach her the gospel, is touched by the spirit, and asks you to baptize her shortly thereafter. The reality is that she easily identifies them as Mormon missionaries through the peephole, so she either hides inside the house or she invites them in for a beer and gets them to question why they're on a mission in the first place.

Subterfuge is not the answer anyway. Open and honest discussions about an easy topic like religion should bring her quickly around to your way of thinking. I hope you've been paying attention in Gospel Doctrine class because you're going to be asked more questions than you ever knew existed about your religious beliefs.

Either you will have a series of inspiring discussions on the topic of religion where the spirit is felt and lives are changed, or you will become a pariah. Actually, that's overstating it a bit. The topic of religion will become taboo, and you will be seen as a pariah when you try to broach the subject. If neither of you will budge from your position, don't lose hope. You can always get married anyway and spend the next fifty years crying yourself to sleep and praying that he'll change. Of course, that's assuming he even wants to get married.

Oh, and don't spit into the wind either.

Relationships

"Relationships… We all got 'em. We all want 'em. What do we do with them?"

-Jimmy Buffet

The Dreaded DTR
(Defining the Relationship)

I was sitting on the floor of my furniture-bereft apartment with Valerie, the first girl whom I had considered considering a girlfriend since my divorce. I had been single for about one year now, and I seemed to have found a little joy in my life, though I was far from being emotionally healthy.

I didn't even know what a DTR was, but I was about to experience my first one. Apparently, four weeks into our dating, it was time to "Define The Relationship."

"David," she started. "I really like you, and I think you like me too." She smiled and squeezed her shoulder up to her head in a little half-shrug. I smiled back and nodded, blissfully unaware of the direction these flaxen cords were leading me.

"I would like to see more of you." Again, I nodded and reciprocated. I really liked her, and seeing more of her would be a good thing. She looked so sweet sitting there. I would be foolish to disagree.

"Do you think we should see each other exclusively?" This was a tougher question. I thought for a moment. Given her last two statements, it made sense to date exclusively. Besides, I'd been looking for over a year and found no one anywhere close to Valerie in any area that mattered to me. She was a genuine, kind, fun-loving person.

"Yes," I answered with a sense of finality. It seemed that this was the purpose of our conversation, and we had come to an agreement. We had, though I was still unfamiliar with the term, Defined The Relationship with relatively little hassle.

I leaned in to seal the deal with a kiss, but apparently, we were still negotiating. "I was also thinking," she continued, "that we should really take our relationship to the next level." She paused, looking as cute as ever. "I think that if we're going to date exclusively, we should be looking at marriage as the end goal of our dating. We should really be committed to each other and take this seriously." Suddenly, I realized that I was being herded in a very specific direction. I noted that her questions were deftly guiding me in a way that would make the captain of Harvard's debate team proud. Had she attended law school and simply failed to mention that little detail to me? She was certainly going for the brass ring on this one.

"Well," I said, stalling for time, "that sounds pretty

serious. I would really have to think about it for a while in order to give you a fair and honest answer."

That's okay," she responded. "I can wait." And she leaned back up against the wall to wait.

"Oh, you want me to think about it right now?" She smiled.

So I thought about it. I mulled and considered. I was thoughtful and introspective. In the end, I decided that if I was going to date Valerie exclusively, it made sense to do so with marriage in mind. After all, that's why I was dating – to find an eternal companion. It's not that we would be engaged; we would just take the relationship more seriously. This was not just casual dating. This was serious. This was a big step considering that my fear of commitment was comparable to a housecat's fear of wolves – primal, deeply seeded, unrelenting, and not unfounded.

After forty-five minutes of thoughtful deliberation, I had a decision. "Yes," I said.

"Yes?" she asked. I nodded. "Yes, you do, or yes, you don't?"

"What? I'm saying that I do want to take our relationship to the next level, date exclusively, and begin thinking about marriage as the eventual goal of our dating." Now I was smiling.

"Oh," she said, her smile now a bit more forced. "That's great." She didn't look comfortable. Something was wrong, but what was it?

I leapt to my feet and pointed my finger at her accusatorially. "You were bluffing!" I shouted. I couldn't believe it. This was hilarious and horrifying at the same moment. *"You didn't think I would agree — not in a million years. You haven't even thought about whether or not this is what you want because you didn't think it would go this far. You were bluffing. I don't believe it. Are girls always bluffing when they talk about relationships?"*

"I wasn't bluffing!" Now she was on her feet. *"I'm just surprised."*

"You were bluffing."

"I'm happy…" Then she kissed me. Argument over. We took our relationship to the next level.

Three weeks after this conversation, she confessed. She had been bluffing.

Two months later, I proved that she had been right in thinking I wasn't ready for commitment by driving our relationship off a cliff like a lemming on steroids.

The DTR is a conversation in which you and your opponent (or dating companion, if you prefer) attempt to Define The Relationship (this is also known as declaring the State of the Union). In all but the most casual of relationships, this is inevitable. There are some delay tactics, but the only way to completely circumvent the DTR is by breaking up. Even that doesn't necessarily work because a breakup often turns into a DTR as you are debriefed by the opposing party. I don't mean to make it sound like a legal conflict — it's actually more like a small skirmish along a hotly contested national border.

While most people dread the DTR, it can actually

be a fun game that allows both parties a chance to develop strategic skills that could come in handy if they're ever stuck in an elevator for several hours with Khrushchev or Karpov (whichever is the former world chess champion, not the ex-Soviet Premier).

When you begin dating someone new, decide if you want to play offense or defense in the DTR game. The offensive player's goal is to define the relationship and it's probable future in clear terms to the satisfaction of both parties. The defensive player's primary goal is to thwart the efforts of the offensive player. If you decide to play offense, your opponent should default to defense. Similarly, if you decide on offense, but your date makes the first offensive move, you'll have to fall back and play defense.

Why, you ask? Well, you can't both play for the same goal. Consider what would happen if you and your opponent both play offense. This means you both want an open and honest relationship in which you both know where you stand and what to expect. If the relationship isn't working, you can both move on without hard feelings. Otherwise, you'll continue to build a relationship of mutual trust and respect, culminating in a long and happy marriage together. Boring! Besides, if that's what you really wanted, you wouldn't be playing games like this in the first place.

If you both play defense, you can spend months, even years, dating, getting to know each other, and having fun, without caring if he's out with someone else tonight, why he isn't returning your calls, or what his last name is. This is what's known as a perfect relationship. More specifically, it is known as a perfect relationship by divorced women, and by men who have never been married. Divorced men, and women who have never married, may see things a little differently. It's a matter of degrees (specifically 180 degrees).

If you decide to take the offensive on DTRs, there are some key points you need to keep in mind:

- Instigating a DTR is seen as a sign of weakness (unless you're as deft as Valerie – and you're not). This puts the other person in the driver's seat. You may eventually have to break up in order to regain control.
- Start conversations by noting environmental cues, such as wedding parties, family sitcoms, and lonely people at the park.
- Make sure that you've thought out where you want the relationship to go before you start drilling the other person for their position. Nothing is more embarrassing than answering a question about a topic to which you have supposedly devoted a great deal of thought and introspection with, "Uhm…"
- Space out your DTR attempts liberally. Weekly DTRs make you look just plain needy and will frighten away anyone who's not equally emotionally needy. If they are equally needy,

however, you may have a bright and satisfying codependent marriage in your future.

- You can only start so many conversations with, "So where do you see this relationship going?" Keep in mind that this is the adult equivalent of, "Are we there yet?" and will be greeted with the same enthusiasm as a backseat full of whiny kids.
- Ultimatums are a great way to get what you want if what you want is to be alone or in a relationship with someone who's easily dominated and controlled.

If you have an unnatural (or natural, conditioned, and justified) fear of commitment, you'll want to jump on the defensive immediately. Keep the following in mind as you run away from everyone who may or may not be your eternal companion:

- Offensive DTR players are often sensitive to the "mood" before beginning an assault. It's pretty easy to keep the mood inappropriate for serious discussions. Avoid the following: radio stations that play soft rock or classical music; restaurants with cloth napkins and employees with French titles (such as maître d', sommelier, and croissant); movies that you watch anywhere but in crowded, public theatres; and romantic walks in the moonlight (unless you're a werewolf).
- Eventually, your opponent will stop waiting for the right moment and try to start a DTR

during an action movie. Don't be rude by acting inconvenienced; just jump into your emergency DTR-out procedure. A coughing fit that takes you out of the room, a bad fall, and channeling the spirit of Sammy Davis, Jr. are all good emergency procedures. You do practice coughing, don't you?

- Beware of the subtle DTRs. Casual comments can be interpreted as statements of commitment. "I love spending time with you," means someone is fishing for the "me too" that means you love spending time with them also. To the offensive DTR mind, it follows that you love them and want to spend all your time with them and they should be shopping for wedding rings.

- SportsCenter is a great way to avoid conversation on any topic. Just look anxiously back and forth between the television and your opponent. Eventually, the problem (your opponent and possibly the relationship) will just go away.

- When all else fails, shoot their questions back at them. Chances are, they haven't thought them through themselves, and will answer, "Uhm..."

Dating Exclusively

Be careful what you wish for. Not only does this old adage ring true, but it's also grammatically incorrect.

You should never end a sentence with a preposition. Frankly, adage makers should know better. My point, however, is that you have presumably been dating in an effort to find someone wonderful to share your life with (when I end a sentence with a preposition, it's okay because I'm exercising artistic license). Now you're halfway to what you're wishing for, in the limbo known as a relationship.

You gave up the excitement of meeting people through blind dates arranged by blind and ignorant friends, dances where you're the only member of your particular generation in attendance, and internet sites where Photoshopped pictures and exaggerated resumes lead to very long first dates. And for what? Well, I'm guessing your relationship fantasy includes romantic evenings in front of a fire, knowing you have a date every Friday night, and thoughtful little gifts just because he loves you.

Hey! Who's that banging down the door? It's Reality, and he wants to have a talk with you. You'd better let him in because you don't want to wait until you're married to listen to him. Reality is your friend, and his point of view should be considered in all the major decisions of your life.

You don't actually have to invite him along on activities with your new relationship buddy. He'll be there whether you recognize him or not. He'll be there when you meet your boyfriend's hippie parents. He'll be there when you realize your girlfriend just lost her grocery money by betting on the Super Bowl. And he'll definitely be there when your significant other tells you he's not allowed into Idaho, but doesn't want to discuss the details.

Reality will be there for you. You just have to listen. His is not a still, small voice. He will scream in your face, "Are you crazy? This guy's been on unemployment for five years! He's addicted to the Home Shopping Network! He does that annoying thing with his toes!" If you don't pay attention to Reality, his screams will haunt your every waking hour for years to come.

If you've faced Reality, had an honest discussion with him about the pros and cons of your new relationship, and you both agree that it bears further investigation, congratulations. You have completely deluded yourself. No, no. I mean you've probably found someone wonderful and should continue to work on building and strengthening your relationship.

Now is the time for your deep-seated relationship issues to blossom forth in an array of colors and emotions that will take you, your beloved, and much of the surrounding universe completely by surprise. That's not completely true. Everyone around you knew that you had trust and commitment issues, they just didn't know how explosive they could be.

How do I know this about you? Well, either you're divorced, or you've been single long enough that you decided to read this book on Saturday night, so you could tell your sister that you already had plans and couldn't fit in another blind date. Don't worry. I'm a retired mental health professional, and I can help you.

Try this classic trust-building exercise. Go into an empty room and close the door. Stand with your arms crossed over your chest and fall straight back, trusting that someone will catch you. What happened? You fell and slammed your head into the ground, possibly causing a concussion which required hospitalization and expensive CAT scans because there was nobody there to catch you. Now get over it and learn to trust somebody, so they can either catch you when you try this exercise, or at least point out how ridiculous it is to slam your head into the ground just because some stupid author who holds no legal liability for your injuries told you to.

Now, what about your commitment issues? No problem. We can fix that too. Buy a cat and lock yourself in a room with it for a week. This will be your life when your children are grown. Did that help you get over it? I thought so.

Of course, now that you're committed to one single, solitary person, all the amazing, attractive, kind, and intelligent singles you've been trying to find for the past five years will come out of the woodwork. It's a trick; don't fall for it. If you hadn't committed to this relationship, they never would have shown up. I don't mean to sound paranoid, but they're simply raving, psychotic freaks disguised as amazing, attractive, kind, intelligent singles in a desperate attempt to ruin your newfound happiness. Either that or they really are what they appear to be, and they're simply trying to save you from the lunatic you've committed yourself to before you make the biggest mistake of your life and marry her. Tough call. I hope you pay your tithing.

Now that you're in a relationship, however, you need to clear your mind of these distractions and focus on the task at hand. That will either be getting to know your partner and establishing the deep level of emotional intimacy necessary for marriage, or sabotaging the relationship, depending upon your point of view. Getting out isn't too difficult. We'll discuss that in the chapter on breakups.

Staying on and building a relationship is a different story. Getting to know your relationship partner is an important task. You don't want any nasty surprises after you're married ("I thought you knew I was on parole"). This is why I'm not a big fan of marrying someone in the same month you meet them. I'm sure you're being objective, rational, and spiritual about the whole situation when you make a decision like this. But are you really sure you're being inspired to get married right now? Sometimes it's hard to hear the quiet whisperings of the still small voice over the deafening roar of hormones and loneliness. Unless you're a resident alien about to be deported, there's no reason not to wait a few months and learn your fiancé's last name. Even if you are deported, true love will follow you out of the country.

Still don't want to wait? Perhaps this short list of "Things You Won't Learn in the First 30 Days of Your Relationship" will change your mind:

- He enjoys farting around you once he feels comfortable.
- He smells really, really bad when he exercises.
- Her sense of humor is inappropriate in mixed company, but she doesn't realize it.
- He resents your kids (because they're smarter than he is).
- That recommend expired in 1996.
- This will be her fourth marriage.
- He thinks he has a couple kids in Arizona, but he's not sure.
- Those great cookies she bakes are really from Sister Fields.
- He can suck in his gut for 30 days.
- She can be very difficult until her medication kicks in every morning.
- There's a reason she won't watch America's Most Wanted with you.

Finally, a Frank and Open Discussion About You-Know-What

If you measure the amount of time you've been single in years, then it's been a long time since… well, you know. This is a serious issue facing LDS singles, so it's important that we, as adults, have a serious and honest discussion about… it.

You spent a number of years enjoying the benefits of marriage, and now that you're single (if you're following the rules) those benefits are no longer available to you. Well, they're certainly available, and that's part of the problem. Although some would suggest that you can't spell "single" without "sin," you lost all your benefits when you lost your marriage (if you want to maintain the values you know to be important).

But once you start dating, and especially when you're in a relationship, you'll find that you miss it even more. It was probably an important part of your life for however long you were married, and it probably will be again when you get married again.

Personally, I'm a big fan, and I've had to find a number of ways to fill the void: chocolate pie, chocolate bars, little chocolate kisses, chocolate milk, cake batter ice cream with chocolate brownies mixed in, and daily exercise. It's a good thing that exercise is such a great stress release because I really, really like "chocolate," and, like many other people in my situation, I need an outlet for my stress. While chocolate is a poor substitute, it won't cost me my temple recommend, cloud my judgment, or multiply and replenish the earth, if you know what I mean.

I once asked my bishop for his official stance on this subject. I presented my case in a thoughtful and logical manner. Surely there were certain allowances within the system of rules and laws to allow for some minor encroachments upon the law for people in my situation (SAMs). After all, I'm not a 16-year-old kid. I was twice that age with a ten year marriage on my resume.

After serious and thoughtful reflection that lasted nearly a full second, my bishop responded with, "No." But to make me feel better, he added, "Ha ha ha ha ha!" I don't know why he thought that would make me feel better, but it didn't work nearly as well as I'm sure he had hoped it would.

In light of this response, the best option is to learn to deal with the loss of something you enjoy. Let's suppose, for the sake of example, that you really like chocolate and have decided to give it up for Lent. No, not Lent (40 days is too short). Let's say that you really enjoy chocolate but have recently developed a severe and potentially life-threatening allergy to this delectable, over-the-counter, carnally-satisfying, depression-abating nectar of the gods. The doctor says that the allergy will run its course eventually, and you will be able to eat chocolate again one day. He doesn't know, however, if it will take one year or ten years for your allergy to fade.

What is the best way to approach the years of your allergy-induced chocolate ban? Should you spend all your waking hours thinking about chocolate, harboring jealous anger towards everyone around you just because they are all enjoying chocolate, often in blatant disregard for their doctor's advice? Probably at first, but this approach will make the years drag out for an impossibly long time.

Perhaps you are considering ignoring the chocolate ban in small ways, trying little bits of chocolate on occasion because the doctor didn't specify exactly what constituted eating chocolate or how much would cause an allergic reaction. Maybe you figure your doctor doesn't know what he's talking about, so you eat as much chocolate as you want whenever you want.

Or do you focus on other things (laundry, your children, exercise, existential poetry), biding your time until the day comes when your allergy subsides? You won't lose your taste for chocolate, or your ability to eat it effectively. Just be sure to marry someone who likes chocolate as much as you do, so that… well, you know. In the meantime, try to avoid the media's obsession with chocolate because that's just going to make things harder than they need to be.

I for one am glad that we were able to get this matter out in the open for the kind of frank discussion that people of our maturity demand and deserve. Honestly, it seems ridiculous that so many people consider the topic taboo and have difficulty expressing their feelings about it in an open and direct way.

The Language of Love / Intergender Miscommunication

Doug: *All the women I know fall into one of two relationship categories: romantic or platonic.*

Angie: *Really? To me you can be friends, good*

friends, friends with romantic benefits, dating casually, dating seriously without commitment, dating seriously with commitment, dating casually with commitment, romantic used to be friends, friends used to be romantic, romantic heading towards friendship, friendship heading towards romantic, romantic heading towards not friends at all, dating exclusively, dating semi-exclusively, engaged, married or divorced.

> *Angie: Hmmm... How would you describe all these?*
> *Doug: Half are black and half are white.*
> *Angie: I suspected as much. What we have here*
are black, midnight, shadow, night sky, dark gray, eggshell, Navajo, pearl, off-white, and white.

While I believe that miscommunication is a much broader field than simply "men vs. women," this chapter focuses on these two specific genders and the gulf that divides their simplest attempts at being understood by each other. You are probably a member of one of these genders trying desperately to understand the other. More likely, your efforts are focused on trying to be understood by the other gender, but that's close enough for now.

Angie's story clearly shows that the depth of intergender miscommunication extends to its building blocks. The different vocabularies of men and women reflect deep differences in thinking. For example, I call burgundy, deep burgundy, and dark burgundy, all red.

This is not because I don't care about their differences. I simply can't see the differences because I'm not an artist.

So when your boyfriend doesn't notice that your relationship has moved from romantic with long-term possibilities to romantic with strong long term-possibilities, don't get angry. It doesn't mean he doesn't care. It means that these distinctions are outside the threshold of his emotional sensory perception in much the same way that elephant rumblings, high-frequency giraffe vocalizations, and bat sonar pings are outside the range of his physical sensory perception. Your dog, however, will sense your distress (or the fact that you had steak for dinner) and move in to comfort you.

This is only a partial explanation of the problem. Years ago, before I realized how little I knew about relationships (now I know, and decided to write a book about them anyway), I was a licensed Marriage and Family Therapist. I learned that marriage counseling most often consists of teaching couples how to communicate effectively. One basic exercise is called reflective listening. The goal is to close the understanding gap that exists between what one person says, and another person hears. A typical exchange might go as follows:

> *Husband:*   *I need a few minutes to unwind when I get home from work.*
> *Therapist:*   *Tell your husband what you think he's trying to communicate to you.*
> *Wife:*   *He's saying that he doesn't want to help*

around the house because he doesn't love me.

Therapist: *Is that what you're saying?*

Husband: *No. I'm saying that I need a few minutes to unwind when I get home from work.*

Wife: *Oh, so you don't want to see me at night? Why do you even come home at all?*

Husband: *That's not what I mean. I'm just saying that I'm stressed and tired after work, and I need about five minutes of watching SportsCenter before I roll up my sleeves and help out with all the household chores.*

Wife (bursting into tears): *But I love you! How can you say that?*

Therapist: *Okay, we still need a little work, but I can sense that we're making some progress (towards what, I have no idea). Why don't you tell your husband something that you would like him to understand about you. Maybe you could explain to him why you're so upset.*

Wife (drying her tears): *I'm under a lot of stress, and I don't feel like he listens to me or tries to understand how I'm feeling. I just want to feel like he cares about me.*

Husband: *Stress? You don't know what stress is. Try my job for a week. Look, I'll hire someone to clean the house once a week. That should prove that I care about you, all your stress will be gone, and I can come home and relax.*

Wife: *That's not what I'm talking about. I mean that…*

Husband (rising from the couch): Looks like our hour's up. We'll stop for pizza on the way home, so you won't have to worry about dinner. And you say I'm not sensitive.

Therapist: *Well, we can't achieve perfect communication all at once. I'll see you at the same time next week.*

Husband (from halfway out the door): Why?

Okay, despite a **slight** exaggeration (for effect), you get the drift of the exercise and the extent to which couples fail to understand one another. It's important to work on understanding what your partner is trying to say because when both parties feel understood, bonds of love and trust grow. Feel free to use that in your relationship – no extra charge.

Each year, thousands of therapists, coaches, and consultants charge big bucks to teach communication strategies in seminars, books, and personal instruction. Because actual communication is so rare, however, I feel that learning to communicate in this way is like being the first person to own a CB. Who are you going to talk to?

Instead, I will focus on the many and varied ways to miscommunicate with your relationship partner. You will learn to recognize these gaps in communication. Thus, you will learn to communicate effectively by avoiding all forms of miscommunication in much the same way that Michelangelo sculpted David by knocking away all the marble that didn't look like a big, naked guy.

Miscommunication: Talking about subjects in which your partner has absolutely no interest or knowledge.

He says: Looks like the Pats will have a tough time tonight. Their QB has a pulled hammie, and the tight end has been on the IR since week five.

She hears: Blah, blah, blah.

He means: It's nice to be dating someone who knows less about football than I do because now I feel like a sports genius.

She says: My mother and sister were shopping when they started arguing about whether *Fried Green Tomatoes* or *Thelma and Louise* was a better movie, and it really upset me because blah blah blah. (Come on. I couldn't even force myself to care enough to make it up.)

He hears: Blah, blah, blah.

She means: I know you don't care about this, but if you fake it long enough for me to get it out of my system, we can make out.

Miscommunication: Asking your partner to lie.

He says: Check out my fancy, new, expensive, completely unnecessary electronic gadget. Isn't it great?

She hears: Will you lie to me to feed my ego? Oh, and can you believe that I convinced myself that is was worth $500 to be able to determine exactly where I am at any given moment and make a phone call at the same time?

He means: Isn't it great? Please tell me it's not just the salesman and I who think I can't live without this because I really can't afford it.

She says: Do you think I'm fat?

He hears: Do you think I'm fat? No, wait! Don't answer that. It's a trap. Just say, "No." Too late. You've already hesitated too long and hurt my feelings.

She means: Will you please tell me that I'm not fat, but in a really believable way, so that I don't suspect for even a moment that you might be lying to me?

Miscommunication: Lying.

She says: Nothing's bothering me.

He hears: Nothing's bothering me.

She means: Something's really bothering me. You

should know what you did, so you had better figure it out and apologize.

He says: I don't even notice other women anymore.
She hears: I'm ready for a serious commitment.
He means: I hope you didn't notice me checking out the waitress.

Miscommunication: Trying to read between the lines.
She says: I don't care what we do tonight.
He hears: I want to make out tonight, but I don't want to seem too aggressive.
She means: I care a lot, and you had better know what I'm thinking, or I'm going to think that you don't love me. Let's see if you've been paying enough attention to be able to anticipate what I would enjoy doing tonight.

He says: I just want to hang out with the guys tonight.
She hears: I specifically don't want to spend time with you. You're crowding me. You're not perfect enough. You don't anticipate my moods. You don't meet my emotional needs. I'm a complicated man, and I just don't think you're sharp enough or caring enough to figure me out and provide

the kind of support that I'm looking for. Maybe a night out with the guys will help me summon the courage to break your heart and sweep you out of my life once and for all.

He means: I just want to hang out with the guys tonight.

Miscommunication: Assuming other genders think like yours.

She says: I had a really rough day.

He hears: Will you listen to me whine for seven seconds and then explain to me how to fix my problem? Be sure to use a condescending tone, and imply that everything would be really easy if I would do it your way.

She means: Will you shut up and listen to me complain for a few minutes, so I can get it out of my system? Then I'll feel much better, and we can do what you want to do. I'll probably even rub your shoulders.

He says: The playoffs start next week.

She hears: There's some sort of sporting event next week.

He means: I won't be seeing you for a while (unless you want to swing by with snack food).

Miscommunication: Letting insecurity or overconfidence filter what you hear.

She says: That's a nice sweater. You look good in fall colors.

He hears: You look good.

She means: Finally, your clothes match. Please let me make your fashion decisions from now on.

He says: You look nice tonight.

She hears: You usually look horrible.

He means: Want to make out?

Miscommunication: Not understanding the context of a statement.

She says: I just need to decide which shoes to wear. Then I'll be right down.

He hears: I'll be right down.

She means: Have a seat. I could be a while.

He says: There's five minutes left in the game. Then we can go out.

She hears: We can go out in five minutes.

He means: We can go out when the game's over. The five minutes of game clock time should pass in about forty-five real world minutes.

Clearly, the source of much intergender miscommunication is a difference in perceptual thresholds. You may be describing your hopes, dreams, and fears in 256 shades of gray or 14 million colors. Unfortunately, your boyfriend can only hear in black and white. Similarly, when he speaks in black and white, and you listen in full color, you're adding colors, shading, highlights, details, and nuances that were simply not intended. The more you attempt to beautify and clarify his words, the further you are from his original, rather simple message.

Individuals communicate in different ways, and I'm not here to say one is better than another (although, clearly it is). They're simply different approaches. It will take both you and your partner working to avoid miscommunication. Blaming communication problems on your partner is simply a case of the pot calling the kettle dark gray.

Breaking Up Is Hard To Do

Original Breakup

Tara: Richard, you're a really nice guy, but I'm giving you
            your ring back. I don't think we should get married.
Richard: Why?
Tara: I just don't think I'm ready.
Richard: That's okay. I can wait.
Tara: I don't think I'm going to change my mind anytime soon.
Richard: We'll see.

1 day after breakup

Richard: Want to go out tonight?
Tara: No, Richard. We broke up.
Richard: We didn't really break up. You said you just need more
            time.
Tara: We did really break up, and it's only been 14 hours.
            I'll probably need more time than that.
Richard: That's okay. I can wait.

1 week after breakup

Richard: So have you thought about it?
Tara: Thought about what?

Richard: About getting married. We could keep our original
date if we started on the invitations now. I'll take you
out to dinner tonight, and we can talk about it.

Tara: We're not getting married, and we're not going out to
dinner.

Richard: Why not?

Tara: Because we broke up!

Richard: What are you getting so upset about? If you change
your mind, we can still work things out.

Tara: I'm not going to change my mind.

Richard: Fine! (Long, awkward silence) Talk to you tomorrow?

Tara: No. Goodbye.

3 weeks after breakup

Richard: How are you doing?

Tara: I'm doing good, Richard. How are you?

Richard: I'm fine, except I was worried about you because you
didn't return any of my calls, so I thought maybe
something was wrong.

Tara: I told you I wouldn't call you back.

Richard: I didn't think you meant it. (pause) I've decided to
give you a little more space, so you can make some
decisions regarding our relationship.

Tara: Thank you.

6 weeks after breakup

Richard: Well?

Tara: Well, what?

Richard: Have you made any decisions?

Tara: Yes. I've studied it out, fasted, and prayed. I've decided that we're not right for each other.

Richard: That can't be right. I've fasted and prayed too, and I'm sure we're right for each other. Maybe you just weren't praying hard enough.

Tara: We're finished, Richard. It's time to move on.

Richard: Just pray a little harder.

Tara: Goodbye.

3 months after breakup

Richard: My parents are in town this weekend. I thought we could all get together and have dinner. They're dying to meet you.

Tara: Why are they dying to meet me? We broke up three months ago.

Richard: Why do you have to be so hurtful? I think you have a lot of issues that you need to look at. I've made a list. If you have a minute, we can go over them.

Tara: Goodbye.

Richard: So should I pick you up at six on Friday? Hello? Hello?

4 months after breakup

Richard: Hey, I have tickets to the game tonight? Do you want to go?

Tara: No, I'm busy.

Richard: Don't be like that. We'll just go as friends.

Tara: The last time we went out as "just friends," you spent the whole evening telling me how stupid I was for not knowing that you're perfect for me.

Richard: That was weeks ago. I'm doing much better now. I'm
dating someone else.
Tara: Hmmmm...

4 months and one week after breakup
Richard: Want to go out to dinner tonight?
Tara: Didn't you get the letter I sent after we went out last
week, specifying in excruciating detail why we can
never see or speak to each other again?
Richard: Yes, but your reasoning was flawed (and frankly
your grammar was poor). I've countered every point
quite convincingly. I'll be happy to go over it with
you at dinner. I can bring your ring. It's not too late.
Tara: Sigh.

And so on, and so on, and so on...

Sometimes breakups go smoothly. Sometimes
they do not. A smooth breakup is when you both agree
that, while you each like the other person for their
many positive qualities, the relationship has reached a
point where it is no longer beneficial for both parties to
continue. For example, perhaps you live in different states,
have radically different life goals, or root for competing
professional sports organizations (you can't possibly be
expected to date a Cubs fan). In this scenario, a sincere
friendship may result from the breakup.

A breakup that does not go smoothly may remind
you of old newsreel footage of the Hindenburg disaster.

Oh, the humanity! You think I'm exaggerating? By failing to recognize the potential consequences of a bad breakup, you commit yourself to a path that will lead to just such a disaster. You must consider exit strategies for future relationships now, or you risk hurt feelings (yours and theirs), legal fees, stalkers, and yet another public apology to the National Forest Service.

Let's say that you've decided to end your current relationship. We'll assume that you have a pretty good reason, such as he smells like a yak (and I'm talking about a lowland yak, not one of those classy yaks from the Mongolian Steppes).

The first thing you need to do is determine if he, as the yak, also feels that the relationship is doomed. You can do this rather subtly by studying his responses as you casually steer the conversation in calculated ways:

- So where do you see yourself in five years?
- Close your eyes, picture yourself in a car, driving down the road of life. Tell me who's in the car with you.
- Everyone who's going to be dating me next week, raise your hand… not so fast, buddy.
- Are you going to be upset if I break up with you later tonight? Should I wait until after dessert?

Now that you've carefully done a little reconnaissance, you know what to expect when you broach the subject. I know you've had an open and honest relationship and you're a good, kind, and honest person. You may still love and respect the person whose heart you're about to crush like a dried up, old leaf. And yet, it must be done. Worse yet, you must lie to him.

Oh, it's true, and it's for the best. You don't believe me? You need to find out the hard way? Okay, go ahead, but don't say I didn't warn you. But before you jump without preparing any little, white lies, let me tell you what's going to happen when you tell yak-boy (let's call him Dave, because everyone will have to break up with someone named Dave at some point in their life) the "truth."

You will tell Dave that you don't want to date him any more, and he will ask for an explanation. "Because, Dave," you will say in your self-righteous I-am-telling-the-truth-so-anything-I-say-is-for-the-best tone, "you smell like a yak."

Dave will be hurt. Dave will be offended. He will tell you that he doesn't smell like a yak, but you will assure him that he does. Dave will go home angry. He will fret and fume and declare that he doesn't need you and your smelling-yaks-where-there-are-none attitude. And then Dave will do something that will make the universe as a whole a little better, but your life specifically much, much worse. Dave will take a shower. With soap.

Yak-boy will drop by your house or bump into you at your favorite lunch spot. He will chat with you casually, a knowing smile on his lips. Finally, he will force you to acknowledge the change:

Dave:	*Well?*
You:	*Well, what?*
Dave:	*Haven't you noticed?*
You:	*Uhmmm… you learned to use a brush?*
Dave:	*No. I showered.*
You:	*Oh (clearly not getting it).*
Dave:	*So I don't smell like a yak anymore.*
You:	*Oh (in mildly encouraging, good-for-you-and-your-hygiene sort of way).*
Dave:	*So we can get back together now.*
You:	*Oh (finally getting it).*

It is at this point that you will remember the wisdom I tried to share with you and think, "Wow. That other Dave was right. I should have listened to his advice. I wonder if he's still single. I bet he'd be a great guy to go out with, and an easy Dave to break up with."

But I digress. The point is that you will realize too late that even though you thought you were doing the right thing by telling the truth, you weren't. You were simply providing the means for Dave to drag it out. If you give Dave a reason for your break-up, he may try to fix what's broken – it's a guy thing (he may not though because it's about him – that's a guy thing too). Then he will approach you with evidence that he has taken care of the obstacle to your eternal bliss and will expect you to shower him with kisses in a fit of love and gratitude. Your response will be, and I quote, "Oh."

This is because you weren't really telling Dave the truth. You were still lying to him. You were lying to yourself too. If the guy of your dreams smelled like a yak, you would either deal with it or tell him to shower. Dave's yak smell was simply an easy characteristic to pick out on a guy that you just didn't like that much.

Now, because you didn't want to give Dave a cop-out excuse like, "I just don't feel like we're right for each other," which, ironically turns out to be the truth, you're stuck with an ex-boyfriend who will approach you every couple of weeks smelling less yak-like than the last time you saw him. He will think that he's winning you back while, in fact, he is simply getting really, really clean (and perhaps developing some hot, new perfume lines for Elizabeth Taylor).

Don't confuse precision with accuracy. You don't have to tell someone why you're breaking up with them because you probably don't know either. Maybe you're right and you simply want a guy with all his original teeth, but maybe you're just not ready for a relationship and you're blaming his toothless grin.

Still can't bring yourself to end a doomed relationship because you know it will hurt the other person's feelings? That's okay. Fortunately, they don't have that same hangup. All you have to do is tap into their cold heart and get them to break up with you. It's really not that hard. Simply develop habits or characteristics that you know are completely incompatible with the social norms of most modern civilizations.

In fact, you don't have to actually do anything. You can simply stop practicing some widely accepted norms of hygiene, such as controlling your bladder. Every time you go out with the person you no longer want to date, have a little accident. Then don't say anything about it. Don't excuse yourself and go to the restroom. Don't try to cover it up. Don't even act like you notice. I guarantee they'll notice, and they'll break up with you faster than you can do your laundry. I haven't tried that one myself, but I have been assured that it will get you out of any unwanted relationship, business or personal.

Myself, I just pick a highly personal and emotionally charged topic and take a hard-line position 180 degrees from my opponent. If they don't want kids, I do. If they like country music, I don't. If they like butter, I insist on margarine. After a short time, the writing is on the wall.

My friend Anne takes this basic principle to a higher, more artistic plane. She refuses to ever break up with anyone. When she senses that this is not the relationship for her, she simply becomes as annoying as humanly possible. She's disagreeable, whiney, clingy, and listens to country music. After about a week of this priming, she sits her victim down and goes into a lengthy speech about how she knows he's the one. Then she proposes. Her success rate is 100%. Every single guy has broken up with her at that moment.

So you see, it is possible to get out of a bad relationship quickly and cleanly. What do you do if you're on the receiving end of, "I just don't think we're right for each other"? There's only one thing to do. You have to take it in the gut, suck it up, and walk away. There's simply no better alternative. Let me tell you a quick story.

The short version is that I fell head over heels for Julie in about three weeks. Everything was perfect, and I could see our future together unfolding nicely. I was definitely counting chickens when all I had were eggs (and I barely had eggs). For some unknown reason, I was convinced that Julie really liked me too. (Perhaps it was the way that she kept telling me how much she really, really liked me.)

What Julie hadn't mentioned was that she was starting to like another guy too – one who happened to live much closer. She wanted to get to know Neighbor Ned down the street better, so she broke up with me. I was shocked and upset, but I walked away with my dignity intact.

Now if the story ended here, it would be a nice lesson in how to gracefully accept an unexpected blow. Unfortunately, I mentioned the minor tragedy to my friend, Angie. She said that Julie wanted me to fight for her hand, and that I had given up too easily. I protested, but she insisted. Against my better judgment (and because I hoped Angie was right), I relented.

I showed up at Julie's house with a lovely gift basket containing items to remind her of our wonderful life together over the past three weeks. I even wrote a poem expressing my feelings, which Angie assured me would melt her heart. (I've now written poetry for two women in my lifetime. The first was my ex, and it's obvious how that went. The second was not much better. I think the romantic impact of poetry has been exaggerated by the media.)

After an awkward moment delivering the package (awkward because the other guy was there), I returned home to await a response. Julie's email sounded more like a restraining order than a friendly, "No, thank you." According to my best recollection, it said, "Don't call me, don't email me, don't write me."

I learned some powerful lessons with this single three-week experience. First, be careful when taking advice. One woman's romance is another woman's stalking. In five minutes, I went from nice guy at the wrong time to scary guy who couldn't take a hint. Trust your own instincts about how to interact with others, unless, of course, your instincts consist of several voices arguing in your head, trying to convince you that your dog is a general in an alien army and should, therefore, be allowed to sleep on the sofa.

Second, you're not going to change someone's mind when they decide to break up with you. And do you really want to? Someone sat down, weighed the advantages and disadvantages of having you in their life, and voted unanimously that they didn't want to see you anymore. Don't argue your case. As soon as you find out that they don't want to be with you, don't waste a single moment trying to convince them that you're wonderful and they can't live without you. They had their chance. Find solace in the fact that they'll never find anyone else as wonderful as you, and one day, when they're old and alone, they'll realize it and regret having cast you unceremoniously out of their lives. And that's only if they manage to survive hurricanes, crocodiles, and other dangers to make it to old age. It's childish, I know. But it works.

Once a relationship ends, take a few moments to reflect upon the person, the relationship, and your interaction. What lessons did you learn that can make you a wiser, stronger, better person? A relationship is only a waste of time if neither of you learned anything from your time together. Here are a few examples of important lessons that you might be able to take from a relationship, or even a single date:

- If he dresses, decorates, and dances better than you, don't ask personal questions. Just move on.
- The local hospital is able to treat someone for a severe allergic reaction to avocados, if you are able to get from the Mexican restaurant to the hospital in seven minutes or less.
- Sushi is an acquired taste.
- If someone insists that you trust them, they're probably not trustworthy.
- You're not allergic to wildflowers, but you're severely allergic to the stings of bees that sometimes come with the wildflowers.

- Don't fall for someone over the phone. They may look way too much like your ex for you to date them without being overcome by huge waves of nausea.
- Anyone who keeps a massage table in his trunk, but is not a professionally licensed massage therapist, should be avoided.
- Nobody's ever just kidding when they make a suggestion, followed by "just kidding."
- If your blind date tries to sell you long distance service, vitamins, skin products, or Amway, it means that your sister's blind-date-loser filter is stuck in the "off" position.

Proposal, Marriage, and Your Second Divorce

My father taught me that a second marriage is the triumph of hope over experience. He said it to be funny, and I suspect that he stole this particular bit of sage wisdom from a stand-up comic he saw on TV. There is, however, wisdom in what he says. It takes a while for hope and faith to gain ground on experience, but eventually they may win out.

Once you've been in a relationship for a respectable amount of time, you'll start thinking about marriage. Keep in mind that some people consider the twenty minutes you spend waiting for a table at a restaurant a respectable amount of time while others think more in terms of the amount of time it takes a glacier to move from one hemisphere to another. The ideal is probably somewhere in between.

If you find yourself on a first date with someone who wants to get married before dessert arrives, you can escape by using any of the techniques covered in previous chapters. If you find yourself agreeing with him, I recommend a therapeutic technique known as "checking yourself into a mental hospital because it turns out that your previous dates were correct, and you are indeed stark, raving mad."

But now you're in a relationship. Let's assume that you've made the spiritual, emotional, and financial investment required to allow yourself to fall in love and hire private investigators to conduct a background check. At this point, I recommend an actual marriage, not a weekend marriage. We've all heard rumors, but I have actually conducted an interview with a woman who was proposed to (on a first date) with, "Want to get married tonight? You'll have to promise me that you'll give me a divorce tomorrow."

While there are a number of concerns with weekend marriages in general, this particular case deserves special attention. First of all, this was a first date. Admittedly, I am not the ultimate authority on etiquette and social norms, but if I have a really, really good first date I might go for a goodnight kiss. While I admire his enthusiasm and optimism, I think he overreached just a bit.

Secondly, this guy didn't even want to be married for the weekend, just the night. My friend found that to be a bit insulting, and an indication that he was not concerned about fulfilling her emotional and spiritual needs through this relationship, but was, in fact, only worried about his own carnal desires. (Shocking!)

Finally, he's trusting someone that he's known for less than two hours to grant him the divorce he wants when he wants it. That's risky. You can certainly see why he's concerned about arranging a clean break prior to the nuptials. Clearly, he's had problems with his overnight brides crying and begging him not to file for divorce because they have fallen madly and irrevocably in love with him over the course of their twelve hours together. Once you've found a good thing, it's hard to let go.

Now that we've established the perils of weekend marriages, let's assume that you're ready to propose an actual marriage (one that you would like to last longer than 48 hours). How should you propose? Remember last time, when you came up with some creative and romantic way to give her a ring and ask for her hand in holy matrimony? Remember how that one ended?

Just kidding. Be cute and creative if you want, but it's probably not really necessary. (Wait. Based on the angry responses I'm receiving from some female editors, it might, in fact, be necessary to be cute and creative. You're going to have to make that call on your own.) Either way, I'm sure that you've already had some serious and detailed discussions about your future together before proposing. If not, you're probably just proposing for the weekend.

Once you propose, and she's accepted (and I can't emphasize the second part enough), you'll need to plan your wedding. If it's a second marriage for both of you, a large and lavish wedding is out of the question. You'll probably want a small ceremony with a few close friends who will be unlikely to mock you. You won't get five blenders this time around, but you probably don't need them. After the wedding, you'll have two of everything anyway. Whether you give half your stuff to charity or put it in storage is a pretty good indication of your confidence in this particular marriage.

Well, you've done it. You've overcome the bitterness, pain, and hopelessness that overwhelmed you after your divorce. You've found someone wonderful and committed to a partnership for the rest of your life and beyond. Enjoy and protect your newfound happiness. During your second marriage, remember all the lessons that you learned the first time around. Maintain open lines of communication, behave selflessly, treat each other with love and respect, and retain your own attorney to make sure the divorce decree is fair and equitable.

But Seriously...

We've taken a lighthearted look at a very serious topic that affects millions of Latter-day Saints. Marriages and families are falling apart at an astonishing rate. In my experience, this tragedy seems more devastating to active church members because LDS teachings and culture can make divorce feel like an insurmountable obstacle. "No success can compensate for failure in the home." So, once I've failed in the home, what's the point in trying anymore?

You may find yourself thinking, "Sure, the pioneers lost their lives or their families in their travels, but they were sealed for eternity. They will be together forever. My forever family is broken, and I don't think we'll be together in the hereafter. Which is the greater tragedy? What's the point in trying anymore?" This is a dangerous trap that we can think ourselves into, but it's simply not true. I'm not arguing with the prophets or minimizing the issue. I'm simply saying that we tend to draw catastrophic conclusions from out-of-context tidbits that we've picked up over a lifetime.

There are scriptural and modern examples of righteous men and women who lost their eternal families and persevered to find joy. Seek out those stories for inspiration in your own life. Remember that while we see divorce as a modern problem for which we have few scriptural and historical examples for education and inspiration, it is not unexpected to Heavenly Father. You might have been blindsided by your divorce, and society may be reeling from the cumulative effects of unprecedented numbers of broken families, but Heavenly Father knew this was coming. He is not without a plan. His plan will not be frustrated. Have faith, be happy, and move forward, knowing that He has a plan, and that He loves you (and your ex, by the way).

At some point I decided that my life was a comedy, not a tragedy. The absurdity of the situation demanded an emotional response, and eventually I got tired of crying and feeling nothing but pain. A thirty-five year old man with two daughters going on a blind date, set up by his loving sister, on which he is actively concerned for his personal safety and that of everyone else in the restaurant because his date obviously hasn't taken her medication today, and no, I don't want to go downtown and get married, and oops, look at the time, we should really get going? Come on. What's not funny about that? You can bang your head against a wall until you lose consciousness, or you can laugh.

Dating creates its own jokes. It's important to try to find someone wonderful, fall in love, and get married again. It can also be frustrating trying to find that someone wonderful, dealing with your own trust and commitment issues, and making a new relationship work. Yes, it's important and serious, but if you take it too seriously, you'll just become frustrated and embittered. Plus, you'll miss the comedy that is your life. Enjoy the process in all of its absurdity.

Have fun, but remember to be careful. Trust your instincts; listen to the spirit. If something doesn't feel quite right about a situation, get out of it. Yes, you may hurt someone's feelings, but you'll be safe. That's more important.

I don't mention children often in this book. That's because I've yet to find any humor in the way children in this situation suffer. The best thing you can do for your children is to treat your ex with respect. Kids deserve to feel like they can love each parent without betraying the other. Love your children, teach them, and allow them to grow. Remember, they have their trials too, and this is certainly one of them.

As you love and care for your children, remember that your Heavenly Father loves you. He wants you to be happy. Do your best, for that is all He expects, and Christ will do the rest.

I don't apologize for the sappy ending. I've tried to use humor to take some of the edge off of a painful situation, but in the end we all need to face our reality and be okay with it. Besides, my publisher made me do it.